Tea With Jesus

- Compact Edition of Daily Bible Readings and Prayers

Sally Demaray Hull

Tea With Jesus – Compact Edition of Daily Bible Readings and Prayers
By Sally Demaray Hull
ISBN-13: 978-1518608810 for CreateSpace Publication
ISBN-10: 1518608817

All Scripture is quoted from the King James Version of the Bible

Front and Back Cover Photos

Website: sallydemarayhullbooks.vpweb.com

Dedicated to my beloved husband
Charlie
I love you
—Sally

Special thanks to Pastor Rick Johnson for his diligence in studying the meanings of various passages used in this book, and then teaching them to us at church.

Each day lists verses and chapters from the Bible to read, which will take you through the Old Testament once and the New Testament and Psalms twice in one year. Readings are listed each day from the Old Testament history, poetry, proverbs, prophets, and New Testament history and letters. In this way, you will be able to read parts of the entire Bible every day, rather than only one portion for days or weeks on end.

Along with the Bible Readings are prayer starters. Each month, ¼ of a four-month cycle is presented on: love, the armor of God, assorted verses on prayer, praying for family members by way of Proverbs 31. Every four months this cycle is repeated.

Lines are provided for writing down your thoughts on the day's Bible Reading or on the prayer starters.

In the back are memory verses. They are arranged according to subjects. Some are individual verses, while others are entire chapters:

Salvation Verses:
(Assorted individual verses)
Verses to Encourage Faith:
(Hebrews 11:1-40; 12:1-2)
The Ten Commandments
(Exodus 20:1-17)
Jesus' Sermon on the Mount Verses:
(Matthew 5-7)
Verses for Worshipping God
(Psalm 136:1-26)
Verses on Love
(I Corinthians 13:1-13)
Verses of Hope
(John 14:1-3)

All quoted Scripture is from the King James Version of the Bible.[i]

January 1
Genesis 1; Psalm 1; Proverbs 1:1-3; Isaiah 1:1-15; Matthew 1; Romans 1
Lord, may my love suffer long. (I Corinthians 13:4)
[The Greek word for charity means love]
 When I am injured, may my love not lose heart, but bravely persevere and endure the troubles. May the thought of punishing or taking vengeance upon my beloved not even enter my mind. May my love take heart, even if times grow hard—even if my beloved offends me. Lord I put on Mercy. (Colossians 3:12)

January 2
Genesis 2; Psalm 2; Proverbs 1:4-6; Isaiah 1:16-31; Matthew 2; Romans 2
Lord, may my love be kind. (I Corinthians 13:14) May it show itself by mildness and kindness. May it show itself by usefulness, goodness, and pleasantness. May my love be virtuous. Lord, I put on kindness. (Colossians 3:12)

January 3
Genesis 3; Psalm 3; Proverbs 1:7-9; Isaiah 2:1-11; Matthew 3; Romans 3
Lord, may my love not envy. (I Corinthians 13:4) May my love not seek to possess what rightfully belongs to my beloved. May it not strive against my beloved, nor be jealous in the sense of wanting to deprive my beloved of any rightful, good thing or person or place. May my love cheer on my beloved in all righteousness, desiring for my beloved to be all that you purpose. Lord, I put on humbleness. (Colossians 3:12)

January 4
Genesis 4; Psalm 4; Proverbs 1:10-14; Isaiah 2:12-22; Matthew 4; Romans 4
Lord, may my love not vaunt itself. (I Corinthians 13:4) May it not set out to display me. May my love not be boastful of myself, but rather may my love seek to display my beloved and boast of him. Lord, I put on meekness. (Colossians 3:12)

January 5
Genesis 5; Psalm 5; Proverbs 1:15-16; Isaiah 3:1-13; Matthew 5; Romans 5
Lord, may my love not be puffed up. (I Corinthians 13:4) May it not be self-inflating and prideful. May it not be a snobby kind of love, but rather, a humble kind—the kind of love that wants my beloved to be seen as the hero of the story instead of me. Lord, I put on longsuffering. (Colossians 3:12)

January 6
Genesis 6; Psalm 6; Proverbs 1:17-19; Isaiah 3:14-26; Matthew 6; Romans 6
Lord, may my love not behave itself unseemly. (I Corinthians 13:5) May it not conduct itself dishonorably, bringing shame to my beloved. May it not be indecent or disgraceful, but rather, full of grace, honour and decency. Lord, I put on forbearance. (Colossians 3:13)

January 7
Genesis 7; Psalm 7; Proverbs 1:20-23; Isaiah 4; Matthew 7; Romans 7
Lord, may my love not seek her own. (I Corinthians 13:5) May it not meditate on me. May my love not make self-centered demands or be aimed at me, but rather may my love seek for the good of my beloved, craving for what is best for my beloved and be "beloved-centered" rather than "self-centered". Lord, I put on forgiveness. (Colossians 3:13)

January 8
Genesis 8; Psalm 8; Proverbs 1:24-27; Isaiah 5:1-19; Matthew 8; Romans 8

Lord, may my love not be easily provoked. (I Corinthians 13:5) May it not be easily angered or exasperated. May it not be easily irritated or become sharp. But rather, may it bravely persevere and be kind. Lord, above all, I put on love. (Colossians 3:14)

January 9

Genesis 9; Psalm 9; Proverbs 1:28-31; Isaiah 5:20-30; Matthew 9; Romans 9

Lord, may my love think no evil. (I Corinthians 13:5) May it not set itself up as a judge against my beloved, judging the bad—but rather, may my love think on the good. When a destructive thought comes, let me immediately think on something constructive, taking inventory on constructive things, which build up rather than tear down. Lord, I put on mercy. (Colossians 3:12)

January 10

Genesis 10; Psalm 10; Proverbs 1:32-33; Isaiah 6; Matthew 10; Romans 10

Lord, may my love not rejoice in iniquity. (I Corinthians 13:6) May it not be glad and thrive over wrongfulness in my beloved. May my love not be full of cheer over injustice or unrighteousness—neither my beloved's nor my own. Lord I put on kindness. (Colossians 3: 12)

January 11

Genesis 11; Psalm 11; Proverbs 2:1-5; Isaiah 7:1-16; Matthew 11; Romans 11

Lord, may my love rejoice in the truth. (I Corinthians 13:6) May it be such a joyous love, that I treat the truth as though it were such a glad thing, that it actually deserves congratulations and I join in on rejoicing. As you, Lord, mingle mercy with truth (Psalm 57:10), when the truth in my beloved is painful to me, may I give my beloved mercy. In this way I can rejoice even in hard truths, for they offer me opportunities to demonstrate mercy and to show love. Lord I put on humbleness. (Colossians 3:12)

January 12

Genesis 12; Psalm 12; Proverbs 2:6-7; Isaiah 7:17-25; Matthew 12; Romans 12

Lord, may my love bear all things. (I Corinthians 13:7) May it protect my beloved like a roof that covers my beloved's faults, hiding them from all that threatens my beloved. Lord I put on meekness. (Colossians 3:12)

January 13

Genesis 13; Psalm 13; Proverbs 2:8-9; Isaiah 8:1-10; Matthew 13; Romans 13

Lord, may my love believe all things. (I Corinthians 13:7) May it be one that has faith in my beloved, choosing to believe my beloved and believe in my beloved, entrusting my beloved with my love and committing to love my beloved. Lord I put on longsuffering. (Colossians 3:12)

January 14

Genesis 14; Psalm 14; Proverbs 2:10-20; Isaiah 8:11-22; Matthew 14; Romans 14

Lord, may my love hope all things. (I Corinthians 13:7) May it be the kind that trusts. May my love be so desirous of a good outcome that it expects it to happen, so much so that it confides in my loved one—it hopes all things. Lord I put on forbearance. (Colossians 3:13)

January 15

Genesis 15; Psalm 15; Proverbs 2:21; Isaiah 9:1-12; Matthew 15; Romans 15

Lord, may my love endure all things. (I Corinthians 13:7) May it remain no matter what. And if need be that it suffer, may my love be the kind that suffers bravely and calmly and not flee away, but perseveres and takes whatever comes patiently and calmly. May my love be the staying-under sort—the sort that holds up my beloved like a supporting wall holds up the roof. May it endure. Lord I put on forgiveness. (Colossians 3:13)

January 16
Genesis 16; Psalm 16; Proverbs 2:22; Isaiah 9:13-21; Matthew 16; Romans 16
Lord, may my love suffer long. (I Corinthian 13:4) When I am injured, may my love not lose heart, but bravely persevere and endure the troubles. May the thought of punishing or taking vengeance upon my beloved not even enter my mind. May my love take heart, even if times grow hard—even if my beloved offends me. Lord I put on mercy. (Colossians 3:12)

January 17
Genesis 17; Psalm 17; Proverbs 3:1-2; Isaiah 10:1-19; Matthew 17; I Corinthians 1
Lord, may my love be kind. (I Corinthians 13:14) May it show itself by mildness and kindness. May it show itself by usefulness, goodness, and pleasantness. May my love be virtuous. Lord, I put on kindness. (Colossians 3:12)

January 18
Genesis 18; Psalm 18; Proverbs 3:3-4; Isaiah 10:20-34; Matthew 18; I Corinthians 2
Lord, may my love not envy. (I Corinthians 13:4) May my love not seek to possess what rightfully belongs to my beloved. May it not strive against my beloved, nor be jealous in the sense of wanting to deprive my beloved of any rightful, good thing or person or place. May my love cheer on my beloved in all righteousness, desiring for my beloved to be all that you purpose. Lord, I put on humbleness. (Colossians 3:12)

January 19
Genesis 19; Psalm 19; Proverbs 3:5-6; Isaiah 11:1-9; Matthew 19; I Corinthians 3
Lord, may my love not vaunt itself. (I Corinthians 13:4) May it not set out to display me. May my love not be boastful of myself, but rather may my love seek to display my beloved and boast of him/her. Lord, I put on meekness. (Colossians 3:12)

January 20
Genesis 20; Psalm 20; Proverbs 3:7-8; Isaiah 11:10-16; Matthew 20; I Corinthians 4
Lord, may my love not be puffed up. (I Corinthians 13:4) May it not be self-inflating and prideful. May it not be a snobby kind of love, but rather, a humble kind—the kind of love that wants my beloved to be seen as the hero of the story instead of me. Lord, I put on longsuffering. (Colossians 3:12)

January 21
Genesis 21; Psalm 21; Proverbs 3:9-10; Isaiah 12; Matthew 21; I Corinthians 5
Lord, may my love not behave itself unseemly. (I Corinthians 13:5) May it not conduct itself dishonorably, bringing shame to my beloved. May it not be indecent or disgraceful, but rather, full of grace, honour and decency. Lord, I put on forbearance. (Colossians 3:13)

January 22
Genesis 22; Psalm 22; Proverbs 3:11-12; Isaiah 13:1-11; Matthew 22; I Corinthians 6
Lord, may my love not seek her own. (I Corinthians 13:5) May it not meditate on me. May my love not make self-centered demands or be aimed at me, but rather may my love seek for the good of my beloved, craving for what is best for my beloved and be "beloved-centered" rather than "self-centered". Lord, I put on forgiveness. (Colossians 3:13)

January 23
Genesis 23; Psalm 23; Proverbs 3:13-14; Isaiah 13:12-22; Matthew 23; I Corinthians 7
Lord, may my love not be easily provoked. (I Corinthians 13:5) May it not be easily angered or exasperated. May it not be easily irritated or become sharp. But rather, may it bravely persevere and be kind. Lord, above all, I put on love. (Colossians 3:14)

January 24

Genesis 24:1-31; Psalm 24; Proverbs 3:15-16; Isaiah 14:1-15; Matthew 24; I Corinthians 8

Lord, may my love think no evil. (I Corinthians 13:5) May it not set itself up as a judge against my beloved, judging the bad—but rather, may my love think on the good. When a destructive thought comes, let me immediately think on something constructive, taking inventory on constructive things, which build up rather than tear down. Lord, I put on mercy. (Colossians 3:12)

January 25

Genesis 24:32-67; Psalm 25; Proverbs 3:17-18; Isaiah 14:16-32; Matthew 25; I Corinthians 9

Lord, may my love not rejoice in iniquity. (I Corinthians 13:6) May it not be glad and thrive over wrongfulness in my beloved. May my love not be full of cheer over injustice or unrighteousness—neither my beloved's nor my own. Lord I put on kindness. (Colossians 3: 12)

January 26

Genesis 25; Psalm 26; Proverbs 3:19-20; Isaiah 15; Matthew 26; I Corinthians 10

Lord, may my love rejoice in the truth. (I Corinthians 13:6) May it be such a joyous love, that I treat the truth as though it were such a glad thing, that it actually deserves congratulations and I join in on rejoicing. As you, Lord, mingle mercy with truth (Psalm 57:10), when the truth in my beloved is painful to me, may I give my beloved mercy. In this way I can rejoice even in hard truths, for they offer me opportunities to demonstrate mercy and to show love. Lord I put on humbleness. (Colossians 3:12)

January 27

Genesis 26; Psalm 27; Proverbs 3:21-24; Isaiah 16:1-8; Matthew 27; I Corinthians 11

Lord, may my love bear all things. (I Corinthians 13:7) May it protect my beloved like a roof that covers my beloved's faults, hiding them from all that threatens my beloved. Lord I put on meekness. (Colossians 3:12)

January 28

Genesis 27:1-29; Psalm 28; Proverbs 3:25-26; Isaiah 16:9-14; Matthew 28; I Corinthians 12

Lord, may my love believe all things. (I Corinthians 13:7) May it be one that has faith in my beloved, choosing to believe my beloved and believe in my beloved, entrusting my beloved with my love and committing to love my beloved. Lord I put on longsuffering. (Colossians 3:12)

January 29

Genesis 27:30-46; Psalm 29; Proverbs 3:27-28; Isaiah 17:1-5; I Corinthians 13

Lord, may my love hope all things. (I Corinthians 13:7) May it be the kind that trusts. May my love be so desirous of a good outcome that it expects it to happen, so much so that it confides in my loved one—it hopes all things. Lord I put on forbearance. (Colossians 3:13)

January 30

Genesis 28; Psalm 30; Proverbs 3:29-30; Isaiah 17:6-14; I Corinthians 14

Lord, may my love endure all things. (I Corinthians 13:7) May it remain no matter what. And if need be that it suffer, may my love be the kind that suffers bravely and calmly and not flee away, but perseveres and takes whatever comes patiently and calmly. May my love be the staying-under sort—the sort that holds up my beloved like a supporting wall holds up the roof. May it endure. Lord I put on forgiveness. (Colossians 3:13)

January 31

Genesis 29; Psalm 31; Proverbs 3:31-32; Isaiah 18; I Corinthians 15
Lord, may my love never fail. (I Corinthians 13:8) May it not be powerless, but powerful. May it not drop away, falling from its position and getting off course. May my love not be ineffective or lose its way, but rather, may it endure all things. Help me Lord, to love this way—to love with your love—agape—unconditional love—love that is not self-centered, but rather, love that is beloved-centered. I commit to love with your love, Lord. Please help me to. In Jesus name, amen. Lord, above all, I put on love. (Colossians 3:14)

February 1
Genesis 30; Psalm 32; Proverbs 3:33-35; Isaiah 19:1-10; I Corinthians 16
Ephesians 6:14 Lord, I put on the breastplate of righteousness. Help me to. No matter what anyone says, no matter how often I fail, I wear your righteousness, because Jesus' blood has washed me of all my sin. I stand before you completely righteous, because of Jesus.

February 2
Genesis 31:1-24; Psalm 33; Proverbs 4:1-2; Isaiah 19:11-25; II Corinthians 1
Ephesians 6:14 Lord I put on the belt of truth. Help me to. You call yourself the truth. You call the enemy of our souls the father of lies. I choose truth. I will walk in truth, because you are truth. The truth is: you are God, I am not. You sent your son to save the world—and that includes me—out of love. Jesus paid for my sins on the cross. The truth is: You love me. And you have provided salvation for me. You have plans for me—good plans—not evil plans. You always provide for me. And you have work for me to do, telling others about you, making disciples. The truth is, because Jesus has washed my sins away, I get to spend eternity in your wonderful presence. In the light of all that, no matter what happens, I will stand firm and not be defeated.

February 3
Genesis 31:25-55; Psalm 34; Proverbs 4:3-5; Isaiah 20; II Corinthians 2
Ephesians 6:15 Lord, I wear the preparation of the Gospel of Peace. Help me to. Help me to recognize the opportunities you set before me to spread your Gospel of Peace. Help me to take courage and do it. Please give me creative ways to do this. Help me to see these souls as you see them. May I be prepared to tell them of the hope that lies in me. Help me to "study to show myself approved unto God, a workman that needeth not to be ashamed, rightly dividing the word of truth." (II Timothy 2:15) May I do all in my power to be prepared. And may you do all that isn't in my power to make me prepared with the Gospel of Peace.

February 4
Genesis 32; Psalm 35; Proverbs 4:6-7; Isaiah 21:1-10; II Corinthians 3
Ephesians 6:17 Lord, I take up the sword of the Spirit, which is your word. Help me to. Your word "is quick and powerful, and sharper than any two edged sword, piercing even to the dividing asunder of soul and spirit, and of the joints and marrow, and is a discerner of the thoughts and intents of the heart." (Hebrews 4:12). You've also said that your word will not return unto you "void, but it shall accomplish that which" you "please, and it shall prosper in the thing whereto" you "sent it." (Isaiah 55:11) May I use your word effectively, in a way that honors you, my Lord and my God.

February 5
Genesis 33; Psalm 36; Proverbs 4:8-10; Isaiah 21:11-17; II Corinthians 4
Ephesians 6:16 Lord, I take up the shield of faith, by which I may quench all the fiery darts of the wicked. Help me to. I know that "without faith it is impossible to please" you (Hebrews 11:6). Thank you for giving me faith in you. You are worthy of all faith. When

the enemy of my soul tries to wound me, I turn to you in faith, knowing that you are God All Mighty, and he is not. You are in control. You have a plan. You will accomplish your plan. You are a good God. Your arm is not shortened. You will succeed in doing your will. The enemy of my soul will fail. I put my trust in You.

February 6

Genesis 34; Psalm 37; Proverbs 4:11-12; Isaiah 22:1-14; II Corinthians 5

Ephesians 6:17 Lord, I wear the helmet of salvation. Help me to. Thank you so very much for saving me, Lord. I get to spend eternity with you! What could possibly compare with that? Just as a physical helmet protects the head, I ask that your salvation protects my mind. You have "not given us the spirit of fear; but of power, and of love, and of a sound mind. (II Timothy 1:7) And as I "have the mind of Christ" (I Corinthians 2:16), help me to use it for your glory.

February 7

Genesis 35; Psalm 38; Proverbs 4:13-17; Isaiah 22:15-25; II Corinthians 6

Ephesians 6:18 Lord I pray in the spirit with all prayer and supplication. Help me to. Thank you so much for prayer. I get to talk with the king of Kings and lord of Lords! I get to talk with All Mighty God! And you delight to hear me. I am unworthy. Thank you for Jesus. Thank you that He made it possible for me to come to you in prayer. Teach me to pray, Lord.

February 8

Genesis 36:1-19; Psalm 39; Proverbs 4:18-19; Isaiah 23:1-9; II Corinthians 7
Ephesians 6:14

Lord, I put on the breastplate of righteousness. Help me to. No matter what anyone says, no matter how often I fail, I wear your righteousness, because Jesus' blood has washed me of all my sin. I stand before you completely righteous, because of Jesus.

February 9

Genesis 36:20-43; Psalm 40; Proverbs 4:20-21; Isaiah 23:10-18; II Corinthians 8

Ephesians 6:14 Lord I put on the belt of truth. Help me to. You call yourself the truth. You call the enemy of our souls the father of lies. I choose truth. I will walk in truth, because you are truth. The truth is: you are God, I am not. You sent your son to save the world—and that includes me—out of love. Jesus paid for my sins on the cross. The truth is: You love me. And you have provided salvation for me. You have plans for me—good plans—not evil plans. You always provide for me. And you have work for me to do, telling others about you, making disciples. The truth is, because Jesus has washed my sins away, I get to spend eternity in your wonderful presence. In the light of all that, no matter what happens, I will stand firm and not be defeated.

February 10

Genesis 37; Psalm 41; Proverbs 4:22-23; Isaiah 24:1-12; II Corinthians 9

Ephesians 6:15 Lord, I wear the preparation of the Gospel of Peace. Help me to. Help me to recognize the opportunities you set before me to spread your Gospel of Peace. Help me to take courage and do it. Please give me creative ways to do this. Help me to see these souls as you see them. May I be prepared to tell them of the hope that lies in me. Help me to "study to show myself approved unto God, a workman that needeth not to be ashamed, rightly dividing the word of truth." (II Timothy 2:15) May I do all in my power to be prepared. And may you do all that isn't in my power to make me prepared with the Gospel of Peace.

February 11

Genesis 38; Psalm 42; Proverbs 4:24-27; Isaiah 24:13-23; II Corinthians 10

Ephesians 6:17 Lord, I take up the sword of the Spirit, which is your word. Help me to. Your word "is quick and powerful, and sharper than any two edged sword, piercing even to the dividing asunder of soul and spirit, and of the joints and marrow, and is a discerner of the thoughts and intents of the heart." (Hebrews 4:12). You've also said that your word will not return unto you "void, but it shall accomplish that which" you "please, and it shall prosper in the thing whereto" you "sent it." (Isaiah 55:11) May I use your word effectively, in a way that honors you, my Lord and my God.

February 12
Genesis 39; Psalm 43; Proverbs 5:1-2; Isaiah 25:1-5; II Corinthians 11
Ephesians 6:16
Lord, I take up the shield of faith, by which I may quench all the fiery darts of the wicked. Help me to. I know that "without faith it is impossible to please" you (Hebrews 11:6). Thank you for giving me faith in you. You are worthy of all faith. When the enemy of my soul tries to wound me, I turn to you in faith, knowing that you are God All Mighty, and he is not. You are in control. You have a plan. You will accomplish your plan. You are a good God. Your arm is not shortened. You will succeed in doing your will. The enemy of my soul will fail. I put my trust in You.

February 13
Genesis 40; Psalm 44; Proverbs 5:3-5; Isaiah 25:6-12; II Corinthians 12
Ephesians 6:17 Lord, I wear the helmet of salvation. Help me to. Thank you so very much for saving me, Lord. I get to spend eternity with you! What could possibly compare with that? Just as a physical helmet protects the head, I ask that your salvation protects my mind. You have "not given us the spirit of fear; but of power, and of love, and of a sound mind. (II Timothy 1:7) And as I "have the mind of Christ" (I Corinthians 2:16), help me to use it for your glory.

February 14
Genesis 41:1-24; Psalm 45; Proverbs 5:6-7; Isaiah 26:1-11; II Corinthians 13
Ephesians 6:18 Lord I pray in the spirit with all prayer and supplication. Help me to. Thank you so much for prayer. I get to talk with the king of Kings and lord of Lords! I get to talk with All Mighty God! And you delight to hear me. I am unworthy. Thank you for Jesus. Thank you that He made it possible for me to come to you in prayer. Teach me to pray, Lord.

February 15
Genesis 41:25-57; Psalm 46; Proverbs 5:8-13; Isaiah 26:12-21; Mark 1
Ephesians 6:14 Lord, I put on the breastplate of righteousness. Help me to. No matter what anyone says, no matter how often I fail, I wear your righteousness, because Jesus' blood has washed me of all my sin. I stand before you completely righteous, because of Jesus.

February 16
Genesis 42; Psalm 47; Proverbs 5:14-15; Isaiah 27:1-6; Mark 2
Ephesians 6:14 Lord I put on the belt of truth. Help me to. You call yourself the truth. You call the enemy of our souls the father of lies. I choose truth. I will walk in truth, because you are truth. The truth is: you are God, I am not. You sent your son to save the world—and that includes me—out of love. Jesus paid for my sins on the cross. The truth is: You love me. And you have provided salvation for me. You have plans for me—good plans—not evil plans. You always provide for me. And you have work for me to do, telling others about you, making disciples. The truth is, because Jesus has washed my sins away, I get to spend eternity in your wonderful presence. In the light of all that, no matter what happens, I will stand firm and not be defeated.

February 17

Genesis 43; Psalm 48; Proverbs 5:16-17; Isaiah 27:7-13; Mark 3

Ephesians 6:15 Lord, I wear the preparation of the Gospel of Peace. Help me to. Help me to recognize the opportunities you set before me to spread your Gospel of Peace. Help me to take courage and do it. Please give me creative ways to do this. Help me to see these souls as you see them. May I be prepared to tell them of the hope that lies in me. Help me to "study to show myself approved unto God, a workman that needeth not to be ashamed, rightly dividing the word of truth." (II Timothy 2:15) May I do all in my power to be prepared. And may you do all that isn't in my power to make me prepared with the Gospel of Peace.

February 18

Genesis 44:1-13; Psalm 49; Proverbs 5:18-19; Isaiah 28:1-13; Mark 4

Ephesians 6:17 Lord, I take up the sword of the Spirit, which is your word. Help me to. Your word "is quick and powerful, and sharper than any two edged sword, piercing even to the dividing asunder of soul and spirit, and of the joints and marrow, and is a discerner of the thoughts and intents of the heart." (Hebrews 4:12). You've also said that your word will not return unto you "void, but it shall accomplish that which" you "please, and it shall prosper in the thing whereto" you "sent it." (Isaiah 55:11) May I use your word effectively, in a way that honors you, my Lord and my God.

February 19

Genesis 44:14-34; Psalm 50; Proverbs 5:20-21; Isaiah 28:14-29; Mark 5; Galatians 1

Ephesians 6:16 Lord, I take up the shield of faith, by which I may quench all the fiery darts of the wicked. Help me to. I know that "without faith it is impossible to please" you (Hebrews 11:6). Thank you for giving me faith in you. You are worthy of all faith. When the enemy of my soul tries to wound me, I turn to you in faith, knowing that you are God All Mighty, and he is not. You are in control. You have a plan. You will accomplish your plan. You are a good God. Your arm is not shortened. You will succeed in doing your will. The enemy of my soul will fail. I put my trust in You.

February 20

Genesis 45; Psalm 51; Proverbs 5:22-23; Isaiah 29:1-12; Mark 6; Galatians 2

Ephesians 6:17 Lord, I wear the helmet of salvation. Help me to. Thank you so very much for saving me, Lord. I get to spend eternity with you! What could possibly compare with that? Just as a physical helmet protects the head, I ask that your salvation protects my mind. You have "not given us the spirit of fear; but of power, and of love, and of a sound mind. (II Timothy 1:7) And as I "have the mind of Christ" (I Corinthians 2:16), help me to use it for your glory.

February 21

Genesis 46; Psalm 52; Proverbs 6:1-2; Isaiah 29:13-24; Mark 7; Galatians 3

Ephesians 6:18 Lord I pray in the spirit with all prayer and supplication. Help me to. Thank you so much for prayer. I get to talk with the king of Kings and lord of Lords! I get to talk with All Mighty God! And you delight to hear me. I am unworthy. Thank you for Jesus. Thank you that He made it possible for me to come to you in prayer. Teach me to pray, Lord.

February 22

Genesis 47; Psalm 53; Proverbs 6:3-5; Isaiah 30:1-17; Mark 8; Galatians 4

Ephesians 6:14 Lord, I put on the breastplate of righteousness. Help me to. No matter what anyone says, no matter how often I fail, I wear your righteousness, because Jesus' blood has washed me of all my sin. I stand before you completely righteous, because of Jesus.

February 23
Genesis 48; Psalm 54; Proverbs 6:6-8; Isaiah 30:18-33; Mark 9; Galatians 5

Ephesians 6:14 Lord I put on the belt of truth. Help me to. You call yourself the truth. You call the enemy of our souls the father of lies. I choose truth. I will walk in truth, because you are truth. The truth is: you are God, I am not. You sent your son to save the world—and that includes me—out of love. Jesus paid for my sins on the cross. The truth is: You love me. And you have provided salvation for me. You have plans for me—good plans—not evil plans. You always provide for me. And you have work for me to do, telling others about you, making disciples. The truth is, because Jesus has washed my sins away, I get to spend eternity in your wonderful presence. In the light of all that, no matter what happens, I will stand firm and not be defeated.

February 24
Genesis 49; Psalm 55; Proverbs 6:9-11; Isaiah 31; Mark 10; Galatians 6

Ephesians 6:15 Lord, I wear the preparation of the Gospel of Peace. Help me to. Help me to recognize the opportunities you set before me to spread your Gospel of Peace. Help me to take courage and do it. Please give me creative ways to do this. Help me to see these souls as you see them. May I be prepared to tell them of the hope that lies in me. Help me to "study to show myself approved unto God, a workman that needeth not to be ashamed, rightly dividing the word of truth." (II Timothy 2:15) May I do all in my power to be prepared. And may you do all that isn't in my power to make me prepared with the Gospel of Peace.

February 25
Genesis 50; Psalm 56; Proverbs 6:12-13; Isaiah 32:1-8; Mark 11; Ephesians 1

Ephesians 6:17 Lord, I take up the sword of the Spirit, which is your word. Help me to. Your word "is quick and powerful, and sharper than any two edged sword, piercing even to the dividing asunder of soul and spirit, and of the joints and marrow, and is a discerner of the thoughts and intents of the heart." (Hebrews 4:12). You've also said that your word will not return unto you "void, but it shall accomplish that which" you "please, and it shall prosper in the thing whereto" you "sent it." (Isaiah 55:11) May I use your word effectively, in a way that honors you, my Lord and my God.

February 26
Exodus 1; Psalm 57; Proverbs 6:14-15; Isaiah 32:9-20; Mark 12; Ephesians 2

Ephesians 6:16 Lord, I take up the shield of faith, by which I may quench all the fiery darts of the wicked. Help me to. I know that "without faith it is impossible to please" you (Hebrews 11:6). Thank you for giving me faith in you. You are worthy of all faith. When the enemy of my soul tries to wound me, I turn to you in faith, knowing that you are God All Mighty, and he is not. You are in control. You have a plan. You will accomplish your plan. You are a good God. Your arm is not shortened. You will succeed in doing your will. The enemy of my soul will fail. I put my trust in You.

February 27
Exodus 2; Psalm 58; Proverbs 6:16-17; Isaiah 33:1-12; Mark 13; Ephesians 3

Ephesians 6:17 Lord, I wear the helmet of salvation. Help me to. Thank you so very much for saving me, Lord. I get to spend eternity with you! What could possibly compare with that? Just as a physical helmet protects the head, I ask that your salvation protects my mind. You have "not given us the spirit of fear; but of power, and of love, and of a sound mind." (II Timothy 1:7) And as I "have the mind of Christ" (I Corinthians 2:16), help me to use it for your glory.

February 28
Exodus 3; Psalm 59; Proverbs 6:18-19; Isaiah 33:13-24; Mark 14; Ephesians 4

Ephesians 6:18 Lord I pray in the spirit with all prayer and supplication. Help me to. Thank you so much for prayer. I get to talk with the king of Kings and lord of Lords! I get to talk with All Mighty God! And you delight to hear me. I am unworthy. Thank you for Jesus. Thank you that He made it possible for me to come to you in prayer. Teach me to pray, Lord.

(February 29 Leap Year)
Matthew 5-7
Ephesians 6:13-18 Lord, I put on the whole armor of God. Please help me to. I put on the breastplate of righteousness, and the belt of truth. On my feet I wear the preparation of the Gospel of Peace. I take up the sword of the Spirit, which is the word of God, and the shield of faith, by which I may quench all the fiery darts of the wicked. I wear the helmet of salvation. I pray in the Spirit with all prayer and supplication. And having done all, I will stand. "For the weapons of our warfare are not carnal, but mighty through God to the pulling down of strongholds; casting down imaginations, and every high thing that exalteth itself against the knowledge of God, and bringing into captivity every thought to the obedience of Christ." (I Corinthians 10:4-5) I "put on the armor of light" and "walk honestly, as in the day; not in rioting and drunkenness, not in chambering and wantonness, not in strife and envying." But I put "on the Lord Jesus Christ, and make not provision for the flesh, to fulfill the lusts thereof." (Romans 13:12-14)

March 1
Exodus 4; Psalm 60; Proverbs 6:20-21; Isaiah 34:1-10; Mark15; Ephesians 5
"I will praise thee, O Lord, with my whole heart; I will show forth all of they marvelous works. I will be glad and rejoice in thee: I will sing praise to thy name, O thou most high." (Psalm 9:1&2)

March 2
Exodus 5; Psalm 61; Proverbs 6:22-24; Isaiah 34:11-17; Mark 16; Ephesians 6
Hebrews 4:14-16 "Seeing then that we have a great high priest, that is passed into the Heavens, Jesus the Son of God, let us hold fast our profession. For we have not an high priest which cannot be touched with the feeling of our infirmities; but was in all points tempted like as we are, yet without sin. Let us therefore come boldly unto the throne of grace, that we may obtain mercy, and find grace to help in time of need."

March 3
Exodus 6; Psalm 62; Proverbs 6:25-26; Isaiah 35; Philippians 1
Isaiah 65:24 "And it shall come to pass, that before they call, I will answer; and while they are yet speaking I will hear."

March 4
Exodus 7; Psalm 63; Proverbs 6:27-29; Isaiah 36:1-10; Philippians 2
Prayer for me to be a good wife/husband/family member to my spouse/family member.

March 5
Exodus 8; Psalm 64; Proverbs 6:30-33; Isaiah 36:11-22; Philippians 3-4
Prayer for my spouse/family member to be a good wife/husband/family member to me. (Praying *for*, not *against*, my beloved one.)

March 6
Exodus 9; Psalm 65; Proverbs 6:34-35; Isaiah 37:1-20; Colossians 1
Ephesians 3:16-19 Lord, I pray that you grant my beloved, according to the riches of your glory, to be strengthened with might by your Spirit in my beloved's inner man; That Christ may dwell in my beloved's heart by faith; that he/she being rooted and grounded in love, may be able to comprehend with all saints what is the breadth and

length, and depth, and height; And to know the love of Christ, which passeth knowledge, that he/she might be filled with all the fullness of God.

March 7
Exodus 10-11; Psalm 66; Proverbs 7:1-3; Isaiah 37:21-38; Colossians 2
Philippians 1:10-11 I pray that my beloved's love may abound in knowledge and all judgment—that he/she may test and assess all things according to excellence—that he/she may be sincere and not hypocritical and that he/she won't cause anyone to stumble—and that he/she will be filled with the fruits of righteousness.

March 8
Exodus 12; Psalm 67; Proverbs 7:4-5; Isaiah 38:1-11; Colossians 3
"I will praise thee, O Lord, with my whole heart; I will show forth all of thy marvelous works. I will be glad and rejoice in thee: I will sing praise to thy name, O thou most high." (Psalm 9:1&2)

March 9
Exodus 13-14; Psalm 68; Proverbs 7:6-23; Isaiah 38:12-22; Colossians 4
Hebrews 4:14-16 "Seeing then that we have a great high priest, that is passed into the Heavens, Jesus the Son of God, let us hold fast our profession. For we have not an high priest which cannot be touched with the feeling of our infirmities; but was in all points tempted like as we are, yet without sin. Let us therefore come boldly unto the throne of grace, that we may obtain mercy, and find grace to help in time of need."

March 10
Exodus 15; Psalm 69; Proverbs 7:24-27; Isaiah 39; I Thessalonians 1
Isaiah 65:24 "And it shall come to pass, that before they call, I will answer; and while they are yet speaking I will hear."

March 11
Exodus 16; Psalm 70; Proverbs 8:1-2; Isaiah 40:1-11; I Thessalonians 2
Prayer for me to be a good wife/husband/family member to my spouse/family member.

March 12
Exodus 17-18; Psalm 71; Proverbs 8:3-4; Isaiah 40:12-31; I Thessalonians 3
Prayer for my spouse/family member to be a good wife/husband/family member to me. (Praying *for*, not *against*, my beloved one.)

March 13
Exodus 19; Psalm 72; Proverbs 8:5-6; Isaiah 41:1-14; I Thessalonians 4
Ephesians 3:16-19 Lord, I pray that you grant my beloved, according to the riches of your glory, to be strengthened with might by your Spirit in my beloved's inner man; That Christ may dwell in my beloved's heart by faith; that he/she being rooted and grounded in love, may be able to comprehend with all saints what is the breadth and length, and depth, and height; And to know the love of Christ, which passeth knowledge, that he/she might be filled with all the fullness of God.

March 14
Exodus 20; Psalm 73; Proverbs 8:7-8; Isaiah 41:15-29; I Thessalonians 5
Philippians 1:10-11 I pray that my beloved's love may abound in knowledge and all judgment—that he/she may test and assess all things according to excellence—that he/she may be sincere and not hypocritical and that he/she won't cause anyone to stumble—and that he/she will be filled with the fruits of righteousness.

March 15
Exodus 21; Psalm 74; Proverbs 8:9-10; Isaiah 42:1-13; II Thessalonians 1

"I will praise thee, O Lord, with my whole heart; I will show forth all of they marvelous works. I will be glad and rejoice in thee: I will sing praise to thy name, O thou most high." (Psalm 9:1&2)

March 16
Exodus 22; Psalm 75; Proverbs 8:11-12; Isaiah 42:14-25; II Thessalonians 2
Hebrews 4:14-16 "Seeing then that we have a great high priest, that is passed into the Heavens, Jesus the Son of God, let us hold fast our profession. For we have not an high priest which cannot be touched with the feeling of our infirmities; but was in all points tempted like as we are, yet without sin. Let us therefore come boldly unto the throne of grace, that we may obtain mercy, and find grace to help in time of need."

March 17
Exodus 23-24; Psalm 76; Proverbs 8:13-14; Isaiah 43:1-17; II Thessalonians 3
Isaiah 65:24 "And it shall come to pass, that before they call, I will answer; and while they are yet speaking I will hear."

March 18
Exodus 25; Psalm 77; Proverbs 8:15-16; Isaiah 43:18-28; I Timothy 1
Prayer for me to be a good wife/husband/family member to my spouse/family member.

March 19
Exodus 26; Psalm 78; Proverbs 8:17-18; Isaiah 44:1-13; I Timothy 2
Prayer for my spouse/family member to be a good wife/husband/family member to me. (Praying *for*, not *against*, my beloved one.)

March 20
Exodus 27; Psalm 79; Proverbs 8:19-21; Isaiah 44:14-28; I Timothy 3
Ephesians 3:16-19 Lord, I pray that you grant my beloved, according to the riches of your glory, to be strengthened with might by your Spirit in my beloved's inner man; That Christ may dwell in my beloved's heart by faith; that he/she being rooted and grounded in love, may be able to comprehend with all saints what is the breadth and length, and depth, and height; And to know the love of Christ, which passeth knowledge, that he/she might be filled with all the fullness of God.

March 21
Exodus 28; Psalm 80; Proverbs 8:22-23; Isaiah 45:1-13; I Timothy 4
Philippians 1:10-11 I pray that my beloved's love may abound in knowledge and all judgment—that he/she may test and assess all things according to excellence—that he/she may be sincere and not hypocritical and that he/she won't cause anyone to stumble—and that he/she will be filled with the fruits of righteousness

March 22
Exodus 29; Psalm 81; Proverbs 8:24-26; Isaiah 45:14-25; I Timothy 5
"I will praise thee, O Lord, with my whole heart; I will show forth all of thy marvelous works. I will be glad and rejoice in thee: I will sing praise to thy name, O thou most high." (Psalm 9:1&2)

March 23
Exodus 30; Psalm 82; Proverbs 8:27-31; Isaiah 46:1-4; I Timothy 6
Hebrews 4:14-16 "Seeing then that we have a great high priest, that is passed into the Heavens, Jesus the Son of God, let us hold fast our profession. For we have not an high priest which cannot be touched with the feeling of our infirmities; but was in all points tempted like as we are, yet without sin. Let us therefore come boldly unto the throne of grace, that we may obtain mercy, and find grace to help in time of need."

March 24
Exodus 31-32; Psalm 83; Proverbs 8:32-33; Isaiah 46:5-13; II Timothy 1

Isaiah 65:24 "And it shall come to pass, that before they call, I will answer; and while they are yet speaking I will hear."

March 25
Exodus 33; Psalm 84; Proverbs 8:34-36; Isaiah 47:1-9; II Timothy 2
Prayer for me to be a good wife/husband/family member to my spouse/family member.

March 26
Exodus 34; Psalm 85; Proverbs 9:1-2; Isaiah 47:10-15; II Timothy 3
Prayer for my spouse/family member to be a good wife/husband/family member to me. (Praying *for*, not *against*, my beloved one.)

March 27
Exodus 35; Psalm 86; Proverbs 9:3-5; Isaiah 48:1-11; II Timothy 4
Ephesians 3:16-19 Lord, I pray that you grant my beloved, according to the riches of your glory, to be strengthened with might by your Spirit in my beloved's inner man; That Christ may dwell in my beloved's heart by faith; that he/she being rooted and grounded in love, may be able to comprehend with all saints what is the breadth and length, and depth, and height; And to know the love of Christ, which passeth knowledge, that he/she might be filled with all the fullness of God.

March 28
Exodus 36; Psalm 87; Proverbs 9:6-7; Isaiah 48:12-22; Titus 1
Philippians 1:10-1 I pray that my beloved's love may abound in knowledge and all judgment—that he/she may test and assess all things according to excellence—that he/she may be sincere and not hypocritical and that he/she won't cause anyone to stumble—and that he/she will be filled with the fruits of righteousness.

March 29
Exodus 37; Psalm 88; Proverbs 9:8-9; Isaiah 49:1-12; Titus 2
"I will praise thee, O Lord, with my whole heart; I will show forth all of they marvelous works. I will be glad and rejoice in thee: most high." (Psalm 9:1&2)

March 30
Exodus 38; Psalm 89; Proverbs 9:10-11; Isaiah 49:13-26; Titus 3
Hebrews 4:14-16 "Seeing then that we have a great high priest, that is passed into the Heavens, Jesus the Son of God, let us hold fast our profession. For we have not an high priest which cannot be touched with the feeling of our infirmities; but was in all points tempted like as we are, yet without sin. Let us therefore come boldly unto the throne of grace, that we may obtain mercy, and find grace to help in time of need."

March 31
Exodus 39; Psalm 90; Proverbs 9:12; Isaiah 50; Philemon
Isaiah 65:24 "And it shall come to pass, that before they call, I will answer; and while they are yet speaking I will hear."

April 1
Exodus 40; Psalm 91; Proverbs 9:13-18; Isaiah 51:1-11; Luke 1
(Proverbs 31:10-13) "Who can find a virtuous woman? for her price is far above rubies. The heart of her husband doth safely trust in her, so that he shall have no need of spoil. She will do him good and not evil all the days of her life. She seeketh wool, and flax, and worketh willingly with her hands." May I do my beloved good all my life and never evil. Help me to look for good things to do—servant things—and do them—willingly. Help me to know that if I am virtuous, I am worthy of being looked for, pursued by my beloved, and that I have value and am not a burden. Help me to be trustworthy—in reality and also in my beloved's mind.

April 2

Leviticus 1; Psalm 92; Proverbs 10:1-2; Isaiah 51:12-23; Luke 2

(Proverbs 31:14) "She is like the merchants' ships; she bringeth her food from afar." Lord, help me to bear the qualities of a merchant ship, carrying things of value—not a garbage scow, which carried garbage. May all that I bring into conversation and all things in life be of value, and not detrimental. May I be personally involved and not expect another to do my part. May I not simply give orders, but bring in the things of value myself. May I be willing and able to bring these things of value from a distance if that's where they are.

April 3
Leviticus 2-3; Psalm 93; Proverbs 10:3-4; Isaiah 52:1-8; Luke 3
Five things to pray for my beloved

April 4
Leviticus 4; Psalm 94; Proverbs 10:5-6; Isaiah 52:9-15; Luke 4; Acts 1
Proverbs 31:15 "She riseth also while it is yet night, and giveth meat to her household, and a portion to her maidens." Lord, help me to be the kind of person who is willing to deprive myself in order that I may give. May I be willing to deny myself extra sleep when someone needs me to give to him/her. I understand that I must rest—but this proverbs 31 woman, after resting her body and mind and soul, got up at the point of having rested enough and denied herself the luxury of resting abundantly, because others had a need for her to get busy and give. May I be this way—resting according to wisdom, but not according to greed. And may I give this way too—according to wisdom and love, not according to greed and self-centeredness.

April 5
Leviticus 5; Psalm 95; Proverbs 10:7-8; Isaiah 53:1-9; Luke 5; Acts 2
Proverbs 31:16 "She considereth a field, and buyeth it: with the fruit of her hands she planteth a vineyard." Help me Lord to give thought and consideration as to what you want me to do, and then put wings to my prayers and thoughts and consideration and do what is in my power to make it happen. And then when it happens, help me to be busy about the work. The proverbs 31 woman thought about it, then bought it, then began using it. It was aimed at fruit-bearing—in her case: grapes. May I aim for fruit-bearing. It may not be a physical piece of land and vineyard, but please open my eyes and means to considering and buying and planting whatever "piece of land" You desire for me to.

April 6
Leviticus 6, Psalm 96; Proverbs 10:9-10; Isaiah 53:10-12; Luke 6; Acts 3
Five things to pray for my beloved

April 7
Leviticus 7; Psalm 97; Proverbs 10:11-12; Isaiah 54:1-10; Luke 7; Acts 4
Proverbs 31:17 "She girdeth her loins with strength, and strengtheneth her arms." Help me Lord, to put on strength and so *be* strength. If I don't do what I can, which is to put strength on—to latch hold of it and make it part of me—how can I expect to be strong? Help me to cover myself with strength, especially those parts of me that no one else sees. If I strengthen those secret parts of me and my life, those parts of me and my life that others see will also be strengthened. Help me, Lord—make me to be strong, both in secret and in public.

April 8
Leviticus 8; Psalm 98; Proverbs 10:13-14; Isaiah 54:11-17 Luke 8; Acts 5

Proverbs 31:18 "She perceiveth that her merchandise is good: her candle goeth not out by night." Lord, help me to perceive correctly and be perceived correctly. I need not worry that the truth shines forth when I have given my best—when I have labored as I should, not being lazy. Then I know that what I have to contribute is good, for I have done my best. So Lord, help me to labor for you, giving you my best—faithfully—even when it costs me.

April 9
Leviticus 9-10; Psalm 99; Proverbs 10:15-16; Isaiah 55:1-7; Luke 9; Acts 6
Five things to pray for my beloved

April 10
Leviticus 11; Psalm 100; Proverbs 10:17-18; Isaiah 55:8-13; Luke 10; Acts 7
Proverbs 31:19 "She layeth her hands to the spindle, and her hands hold the distaff." Lord help me to begin and then to continue on in whatever you call me to do. May I be willing to get personally involved—laying my hands on this work—touching it myself—pressing into it in commitment as I hold it and so make it mine—my work for Your glory, which is really Yours entrusted to me. May I do what You set before me to do.

April 11
Leviticus 12; Psalm 101; Proverbs 10:19-20; Isaiah 56:1-8; Luke 11; Acts 8
Proverbs 31:20 "She stretcheth out her hand to the poor; yea, she reacheth forth her hands to the needy." Help me Lord, to live a life that is purposely reaching out to those in need—personally reaching out—not *only* writing a check for those who reach out, but in addition to writing a check, to do this *myself* also. Help me to touch—that personal involvement—the poor and the needy. Help me to see who are poor and who are needy and not just assume that I know already. Some have needs that go beyond money. Some are poor even though they have thousands in the bank. Help me to reach out to them.

April 12
Leviticus 13; Psalm 102; Proverbs 10:21-22; Isaiah 56:9-12; Luke 12; Acts 9
Five things to pray for my beloved

April 13
Leviticus 14; Psalm 103; Proverbs 10:23-24; Isaiah 57:1-12; Luke 13; Acts 10
Proverbs 31:21 "She is not afraid of the snow for her household: for all her household are clothed with scarlet." Lord, help me to live my life in such a way that I will have no reason to fear for my household, no matter what comes. As much as depends on me, may I be faithful to do it, and leave the rest in Your hands, that I be not afraid for my household, knowing that I have done my part, and that You will do Yours. Thank You Lord.

April 14
Leviticus 15; Psalm 104; Proverbs 10:25-26; Isaiah 57:13-21; Luke 14; Acts 11
Proverbs 31:22 "She maketh herself coverings of tapestry; her clothing is silk and purple." Help me, Lord, to make things with my own hands and give it my best. This proverbs 31 woman made clothing for herself and it was the best. It was silk and the sought-after, valuable "purple". Help me to remember that it's alright if I have something of value and that it's alright to spend time on making something for me. Help me not to confuse a servant's heart with thinking I'm of no value. You gave Your Son for me, showing me that You find me valuable. Thank You Lord.

April 15
Leviticus 16; Psalm 105; Proverbs 10:27-28; Isaiah 58:1-7; Luke 15; Acts 12
Five things to pray for my beloved

April 16
Leviticus 17; Psalm 106; Proverbs 10:29-30; Isaiah 58:8-14; Luke 16; Acts 13
Proverbs 31:23 "Her husband is known in the gates, when he sitteth among the elders of the land." Lord may my life be lived in such a way that I not only bring glory to You, but also to my beloved, especially when he/she is out and about in the public eye. May he/she be known in a good and positive way, among those who have wisdom and authority. And may I have a hand in this, doing all in my power to promote him/her—ultimately for Your honor and glory, but also for my beloved's.

April 17
Leviticus 18; Psalm 107; Proverbs 10:31-32; Isaiah 59:1-8; Luke 17; Acts 14
Proverbs 31:24 "She maketh fine linen, and selleth it; and delivereth girdles unto the merchant." Lord, help me to make whatever You've given me the talent and means of making. And may I do it for Your glory. But may I not stop there, but take it to the next step and sell it—whether literally or figuratively—receiving from the blessings You mean for me to have from it. And may I use these blessings the way You intend. And finally, help me to deliver to others whatever it is You've given me the ability to do and make, that the blessings will not stop, but will be passed along. Help me to give You my best.

April 18
Leviticus 19; Psalm 108; Proverbs 11:1-2; Isaiah 59:9-21; Luke 18; Acts 15
Five things to pray for my beloved

April 19
Leviticus 20; Psalm 109; Proverbs 11:3-4; Isaiah 60:1-11; Luke 19; Acts 16
Proverbs 31:25 "Strength and honour are her clothing; and she shall rejoice in time to come." Lord, help me to be the person You created me to be. May I be a person of strength and honor. May my strength and honor cover me like clothing covers my body—touching all of me—covering what is private, but not taking it away—enhancing what is public, giving it beauty and grace and an artistic look. May my strength and honor be in You. The joy of the Lord is my strength (Nehemiah 8:10). And being clothed in strength and honor, may I rejoice. Even if today is hard, help me to remember that I will rejoice in time to come—for "weeping may endure for a night, but joy cometh in the morning." (Psalm 30:5)

April 20
Leviticus 21; Psalm 110; Proverbs 11:5-6; Isaiah 60:12-22; Luke 20; Acts 17
Proverbs 31:26 "She openeth her mouth with wisdom; and in her tongue is the law of kindness." Lord, may I have a kind tongue and use it wisely. May I remember to use it and not stay silent all the time. But in using it, may I use wisdom and kindness—both of which know that there is a right timing and a right choice of words and tone of voice that when all combined together make for wise and kind speech. Help me so to speak.

April 21
Leviticus 22; Psalm 111; Proverbs 11:7-8; Isaiah 61:1-6; Luke 21; Acts 18
Five things to pray for my beloved

April 22
Leviticus 23; Psalm 112; Proverbs 11:9-10; Isaiah 61:7-11; Luke 22; Acts 19
Proverbs 31:27 "She looketh well to the ways of her household, and eateth not the bread of idleness." Lord, help me to be observant where my household is concerned. Help me to purposefully look and notice everything that concerns my household. And may I not stop with the looking and observing, but may I act upon what I observe and

not be idle. May I not allow things to slip by. But may I do what needs to be done, even when I don't feel like it for one reason or another. Help me not to cultivate idleness.

April 23

Leviticus 24; Psalm 113; Proverbs 11:11-12; Isaiah 62:1-7; Luke 23; Acts 20

Proverbs 31:28 "Her children arise up, and call her blessed; her husband also, and he praiseth her." Whether children of my body or children of my ministry, or children of my heart, whether they are near or far, teach me how to pray in regard to them. Lord may I live every day in such a way as being deserving of having the children rise up and call me blessed.

April 24

Leviticus 25; Psalm 114; Proverbs 11:13-14; Isaiah 62:8-12; Luke 24; Acts 21

Five things to pray for my beloved

April 25

Leviticus 26; Psalm 115; Proverbs 11:15-16; Isaiah 63:1-9; Acts 22

Proverbs 31:28 "Her children arise up, and call her blessed; her husband also, and he praiseth her." May I *be* all that I am supposed to be, so as to be deserving of my beloved's praise and the children's blessings—whether or not they give it to me. Please help me to live so closely to You that I will be deserving of their blessings and praises, but not worry about whether or not they give it to me. May I leave that to be between You and them.

April 26

Leviticus 27; Psalm 116; Proverbs 11:17-18; Isaiah 63:10-19; Acts 23

Proverbs 31:29 "Many daughters have done virtuously, but thou excellest them all." Lord, when all is said and done, all that is going to matter is You and how we lived virtuously. May I live my life virtuously for You. May I do such a good job at it, that when compared to others, I will excel them all—not so that I can be number one—but that my aim will be to be as virtuous as You created me to be—and that all of us will so strive. May I succeed, Lord. May I not see myself as a failure and as less, but as one who is virtuous—and this is the place of excelling them all: in virtue. May I never forget the value of virtue.

April 27

Numbers 1; Psalm 117; Proverbs 11:19-20; Isaiah 64:1-6; Acts 24

Five things to pray for my beloved

April 28

Numbers 2; Psalm 118; Proverbs 11:21-22; Isaiah 64:7-12; Acts 25

Proverbs 31:30 "Favour is deceitful, and beauty is vain: but a woman that feareth the LORD, she shall be praised." Lord, help me to discern between what is real and what is empty. May I not concentrate on illusions like favor and beauty. At best, these are only momentary. But instead, may I spend my life and all that I am and have in fearing You—holding You in awesome esteem, for You are my God. And may I allow this very thing to be my praise.

April 29

Numbers 3; Psalm 119:1-40; Proverbs 11:23-24; Isaiah 65:1-10; Acts 26

Proverbs 31:31 "Give her of the fruit of her hands; and let her own works praise her in the gates." Lord, please give me fruit. You've promised that the righteous will still bear fruit in old age (Psalm 92:14). This is my heart's desire—that I will never stop bearing fruit unto You until you call me home. May this fruit be my praise—not *me* but my *fruit*. May my fruit take me to the places of influence, wherever You would have me to go.

April 30

Numbers 4; Psalm 119:41-88; Proverbs 11:25-26; Isaiah 65:11-25; Acts 27
Five things to pray for my beloved
May 1
Numbers 5; Psalm 119:89-136; Proverbs 11:27-28; Isaiah 66:1-12; Acts 28
Lord, may my love suffer long. (I Corinthian 13:4)
[The Greek word for charity means love]
When I am injured, may my love not lose heart, but bravely persevere and endure the troubles. May the thought of punishing or taking vengeance upon my beloved not even enter my mind. May my love take heart, even if times grow hard—even if my beloved offends me. Lord I put on mercy. (Colossians 3:12)
May 2
Numbers 6; Psalm 119:137-176; Proverbs 11:29-31; Isaiah 66:13-24; Hebrews 1
Lord, may my love be kind. (I Corinthians 13:14) May it show itself by mildness and kindness. May it show itself by usefulness, goodness, and pleasantness. May my love be virtuous. Lord, I put on kindness. (Colossians 3:12)
May 3
Numbers 7; Job 1; Proverbs 12:1-2; Jeremiah 1:1-10; Hebrews 2
Lord, may my love not envy. (I Corinthians 13:4) May my love not seek to possess what rightfully belongs to my beloved. May it not strive against my beloved, nor be jealous in the sense of wanting to deprive my beloved of any rightful, good thing or person or place. May my love cheer on my beloved in all righteousness, desiring for my beloved to be all that you purpose. Lord, I put on humbleness. (Colossians 3:12)
May 4
Numbers 8; Job 2; Proverbs 12:3-4; Jeremiah 1:11-19; Hebrews 3
Lord, may my love not vaunt itself. (I Corinthians 13:4) May it not set out to display me. May my love not be boastful of myself, but rather may my love seek to display my beloved and boast of him. Lord, I put on meekness. (Colossians 3:12)
May 5
Numbers 9; Job 3; Proverbs 12:5-6; Jeremiah 2:1-19; Hebrews 4
Lord, may my love not be puffed up. (I Corinthians 13:4) May it not be self-inflating and prideful. May it not be a snobby kind of love, but rather, a humble kind—the kind of love that wants my beloved to be seen as the hero of the story instead of me. Lord, I put on longsuffering. (Colossians 3:12)
May 6
Numbers 10; Job 4; Proverbs 12:7-8; Jeremiah 2:20-37; Hebrews 5
Lord, may my love not behave itself unseemly. (I Corinthians 13:5) May it not conduct itself dishonorably, bringing shame to my beloved. May it not be indecent or disgraceful, but rather, full of grace, honour and decency. Lord, I put on forbearance. (Colossians 3:13)
May 7
Numbers 11; Job 5; Proverbs 12:9-10; Jeremiah 3:1-11; Hebrews 6
Lord, may my love not seek her own. (I Corinthians 13:5) May it not meditate on me. May my love not make self-centered demands or be aimed at me, but rather may my love seek for the good of my beloved, craving for what is best for my beloved and be "beloved-centered" rather than "self-centered". Lord, I put on forgiveness. (Colossians 3:13)
May 8
Numbers 12; Job 6; Proverbs 12:11-13; Jeremiah 3:12-25; Hebrews 7

Lord, may my love not be easily provoked. (I Corinthians 13:5) May it not be easily angered or exasperated. May it not be easily irritated or become sharp. But rather, may it bravely persevere and be kind. Lord, above all, I put on love. (Colossians 3:14)

May 9
Numbers 13; Job 7; Proverbs 12:14-15; Jeremiah 4:1-18; Hebrews 8
Lord, may my love think no evil. (I Corinthians 13:5) May it not set itself up as a judge against my beloved, judging the bad—but rather, may my love think on the good. When a destructive thought comes, let me immediately think on something constructive, taking inventory on constructive things, which build up rather than tear down. Lord, I put on mercy. (Colossians 3:12)

May 10
Numbers 14; Job 8; Proverbs 12:16-18; Jeremiah 4:19-31; Hebrews 9
Lord, may my love not rejoice in iniquity. (I Corinthians 13:6) May it not be glad and thrive over wrongfulness in my beloved. May my love not be full of cheer over injustice or unrighteousness—neither my beloved's nor my own. Lord I put on kindness. (Colossians 3: 12)

May 11
Numbers 15; Job 9; Proverbs 12:19-20; Jeremiah 5:1-18; Hebrews 10
Lord, may my love rejoice in the truth (I Corinthians 13:6) May it be such a joyous love, that I treat the truth as though it were such a glad thing, that it actually deserves congratulations and I join in on rejoicing. As you, Lord, mingle mercy with truth (Psalm 57:10), when the truth in my beloved is painful to me, may I give my beloved mercy. In this way I can rejoice even in hard truths, for they offer me opportunities to demonstrate mercy and to show love. Lord I put on humbleness. (Colossians 3:12)

May 12
Numbers 16; Job 10; Proverbs 12:21-23; Jeremiah 5:19-31; Hebrews 11
Lord, may my love bear all things (I Corinthians 13:7) May it protect my beloved like a roof that covers my beloved's faults, hiding them from all that threatens my beloved. Lord I put on meekness. (Colossians 3:12)

May 13
Numbers 17; Job 11; Proverbs 12:24-25; Jeremiah 6:1-15; Hebrews 12
Lord, may my love believe all things (I Corinthians 13:7) May it be one that has faith in my beloved, choosing to believe my beloved and believe in my beloved, entrusting my beloved with my love and committing to love my beloved. Lord I put on longsuffering. (Colossians 3:12)

May 14
Numbers 18; Job 12; Proverbs 12:26-28; Jeremiah 6:16-30; Hebrews 13
Lord, may my love hope all things (I Corinthians 13:7) May it be the kind that trusts. May my love be so desirous of a good outcome that it expects it to happen, so much so that it confides in my loved one—it hopes all things. Lord I put on forbearance. (Colossians 3:13)

May 15
Numbers 19; Job 13; Proverbs 13:1-2; Jeremiah 7:1-16; John 1
Lord, may my love endure all things. (I Corinthians 13:7) May it remain no matter what. And if need be that it suffer, may my love be the kind that suffers bravely and calmly and not flee away, but perseveres and takes whatever comes patiently and calmly. May my love be the staying-under sort—the sort that holds up my beloved like a supporting wall holds up the roof. May it endure. Lord I put on forgiveness. (Colossians 3:13)

May 16
Numbers 20; Job 14; Proverbs 13:3-6; Jeremiah 7:17-34; John 2
Lord, may my love suffer long. (I Corinthian 13:4) When I am injured, may my love not lose heart, but bravely persevere and endure the troubles. May the thought of punishing or taking vengeance upon my beloved not even enter my mind. May my love take heart, even if times grow hard—even if my beloved offends me. Lord I put on mercy. (Colossians 3:12)

May 17
Numbers 21; Job 15; Proverbs 13:7-8; Jeremiah 8:1-12; John 3
Lord, may my love be kind. (I Corinthians 13:14) May it show itself by mildness and kindness. May it show itself by usefulness, goodness, and pleasantness. May my love be virtuous. Lord, I put on kindness.
(Colossians 3:12)

May 18
Numbers 22; Job 16; Proverbs 13:9-11; Jeremiah 8:13-22; John 4
Lord, may my love not envy. (I Corinthians 13:4) May my love not seek to possess what rightfully belongs to my beloved. May it not strive against my beloved, nor be jealous in the sense of wanting to deprive my beloved of any rightful, good thing or person or place. May my love cheer on my beloved in all righteousness, desiring for my beloved to be all that you purpose. Lord, I put on humbleness. (Colossians 3:12)

May 19
Numbers 23; Job 17; Proverbs 13:12-13; Jeremiah 9:1-11; John 5; James 1
Lord, may my love not vaunt itself. (I Corinthians 13:4) May it not set out to display me. May my love not be boastful of myself, but rather may my love seek to display my beloved and boast of him/her. Lord, I put on meekness. (Colossians 3:12)

May 20
Numbers 24; Job 18; Proverbs 13:14-16; Jeremiah 9:12-26; John 6; James 2
Lord, may my love not be puffed up. (I Corinthians 13:4) May it not be self-inflating and prideful. May it not be a snobby kind of love, but rather, a humble kind—the kind of love that wants my beloved to be seen as the hero of the story instead of me. Lord, I put on longsuffering. (Colossians 3:12)

May 21
Numbers 25; Job 19; Proverbs 13:17-18; Jeremiah 10:1-16; John 7; James 3
Lord, may my love not behave itself unseemly. (I Corinthians 13:5) May it not conduct itself dishonorably, bringing shame to my beloved. May it not be indecent or disgraceful, but rather, full of grace, honour and decency. Lord, I put on forbearance. (Colossians 3:13)

May 22
Numbers 26; Job 20; Proverbs 13:19-21; Jeremiah 10:17-25; John 8; James 4
Lord, may my love not seek her own. (I Corinthians 13:5) May it not meditate on me. May my love not make self-centered demands or be aimed at me, but rather may my love seek for the good of my beloved, craving for what is best for my beloved and be "beloved-centered" rather than "self-centered". Lord, I put on forgiveness. (Colossians 3:13)

May 23
Numbers 27; Job 21; Proverbs 13:22-23; Jeremiah 11:1-10; John 9; James 5

Lord, may my love not be easily provoked. (I Corinthians 13:5) May it not be easily angered or exasperated. May it not be easily irritated or become sharp. But rather, may it bravely persevere and be kind. Lord, above all, I put on love. (Colossians 3:14)

May 24
Numbers 28; Job 22; Proverbs 13:24-25; Jeremiah 11:11-23; John 10; I Peter 1
Lord, may my love think no evil. (I Corinthians 13:5) May it not set itself up as a judge against my beloved, judging the bad—but rather, may my love think on the good. When a destructive thought comes, let me immediately think on something constructive, taking inventory on constructive things, which build up rather than tear down. Lord, I put on mercy. (Colossians 3:12)

May 25
Numbers 29; Job 23; Proverbs 14:1-3; Jeremiah 12:1-6; John 11; I Peter 2
Lord, may my love not rejoice in iniquity. (I Corinthians 13:6) May it not be glad and thrive over wrongfulness in my beloved. May my love not be full of cheer over injustice or unrighteousness—neither my beloved's nor my own. Lord I put on kindness (Colossians 3: 12)

May 26
Numbers 30; Job 24; Proverbs 14:4-5; Jeremiah 12:7-17; John 12; I Peter 3
Lord, may my love rejoice in the truth (I Corinthians 13:6) May it be such a joyous love, that I treat the truth as though it were such a glad thing, that it actually deserves congratulations and I join in on rejoicing. As you, Lord, mingle mercy with truth (Psalm 57:10), when the truth in my beloved is painful to me, may I give my beloved mercy. In this way I can rejoice even in hard truths, for they offer me opportunities to demonstrate mercy and to show love. Lord I put on humbleness. (Colossians 3:12)

May 27
Numbers 31; Job 25-26; Proverbs 14:6-8; Jeremiah 13:1-14; John 13; I Peter 4
Lord, may my love bear all things. (I Corinthians 13:7) May it protect my beloved like a roof that covers my beloved's faults, hiding them from all that threatens my beloved. Lord I put on meekness. (Colossians 3:12)

May 28
Numbers 32; Job 27; Proverbs 14:9-10; Jeremiah 13:15-27; John 14; I Peter 5
Lord, may my love believe all things (I Corinthians 13:7) May it be one that has faith in my beloved, choosing to believe my beloved and believe in my beloved, entrusting my beloved with my love and committing to love my beloved. Lord I put on longsuffering. (Colossians 3:12)

May 29
Numbers 33; Job 28; Proverbs 14:11-13; Jeremiah 14:1-12; John 15; II Peter 1
Lord, may my love hope all things (I Corinthians 13:7) May it be the kind that trusts. May my love be so desirous of a good outcome that it expects it to happen, so much so that it confides in my loved one—it hopes all things. Lord I put on forbearance. (Colossians 3:13

May 30
Numbers 34; Job 29; Proverbs 14:14-15; Jeremiah 14:13-22; John 16; II Peter 2
Lord, may my love endure all things. (I Corinthians 13:7) May it remain no matter what. And if need be that it suffer, may my love be the kind that suffers bravely and calmly and not flee away, but perseveres and takes whatever comes patiently and calmly. May my love be the staying-under sort—the sort that holds up my beloved like a supporting wall holds up a roof. May it endure. Lord I put on forgiveness. (Colossians 3:13)

May 31
Numbers 35; Job 30; Proverbs 14:16-18; Jeremiah 15:1-9; John 17; II Peter 3
(I Corinthians 13:4-8 KJV – the word love has been substituted for the word charity)
"Love suffereth long, and is kind; love envieth not; love vaunteth not itself, is not puffed up, Doth not behave itself unseemly, seeketh not her own, is not easily provoked, thinketh no evil; Rejoiceth not in iniquity, but rejoiceth in the truth; Beareth all things, believeth all things, hopeth all things, endureth all things. Love never faileth." Help me to put on mercy, kindness, humbleness, meekness, longsuffering, forbearance and forgiveness, and above all: love. (Colossians 3:12-14)

June 1
Numbers 36; Job 31; Proverbs 14:19-20; Jeremiah 15:10-21; John 18; I John 1
Ephesians 6:14 Lord, I put on the breastplate of righteousness. Help me to. No matter what anyone says, no matter how often I fail, I wear your righteousness, because Jesus' blood has washed me of all my sin. I stand before you completely righteous, because of Jesus.

June 2
Deuteronomy 1; Job 32; Proverbs 14:21-23; Jeremiah 16:1-9; John 19; I John 2
Ephesians 6:14 Lord I put on the belt of truth. Help me to. You call yourself the truth. You call the enemy of our souls the father of lies. I choose truth. I will walk in truth, because you are truth. The truth is: you are God, I am not. You sent your son to save the world—and that includes me—out of love. Jesus paid for my sins on the cross. The truth is: You love me. And you have provided salvation for me. You have plans for me—good plans—not evil plans. You always provide for me. And you have work for me to do, telling others about you, making disciples. The truth is, because Jesus has washed my sins away, I get to spend eternity in your wonderful presence. In the light of all that, no matter what happens, I will stand firm and not be defeated.

June 3
Deuteronomy 2; Job 33; Proverbs 14:24-25; Jeremiah 16:10-21; John 20; I John 3
Ephesians 6:15 Lord, I wear the preparation of the Gospel of Peace. Help me to. Help me to recognize the opportunities you set before me to spread your Gospel of Peace. Help me to take courage and do it. Please give me creative ways to do this. Help me to see these souls as you see them. May I be prepared to tell them of the hope that lies in me. Help me to "study to show myself approved unto God, a workman that needeth not to be ashamed, rightly dividing the word of truth." (II Timothy 2:15) May I do all in my power to be prepared. And may you do all that isn't in my power to make me prepared with the Gospel of Peace.

June 4
Deuteronomy 3; Job 34; Proverbs 14:26-28; Jeremiah 17:1-18; John 21; I John 4
Ephesians 6:17 Lord, I take up the sword of the Spirit, which is your word. Help me to. Your word "is quick and powerful, and sharper than any two edged sword, piercing even to the dividing asunder of soul and spirit, and of the joints and marrow, and is a discerner of the thoughts and intents of the heart." (Hebrews 4:12). You've also said that your word will not return unto you "void, but it shall accomplish that which" you "please, and it shall prosper in the thing whereto" you "sent it." (Isaiah 55:11) May I use your word effectively, in a way that honors you, my Lord and my God.

June 5
Deuteronomy 4; Job 35; Proverbs 14:29-30; Jeremiah 17:19-27; I John 5
Ephesians 6:16 Lord, I take up the shield of faith, by which I may quench all the fiery darts of the wicked. Help me to. I know that "without faith it is impossible to please" you

(Hebrews 11:6). Thank you for giving me faith in you. You are worthy of all faith. When the enemy of my soul tries to wound me, I turn to you in faith, knowing that you are God All Mighty, and he is not. You are in control. You have a plan. You will accomplish your plan. You are a good God. Your arm is not shortened. You will succeed in doing your will. The enemy of my soul will fail. I put my trust in You.

June 6

Deuteronomy 5; Job 36; Proverbs 14:31-33; Jeremiah 18:1-10; II John

Ephesians 6:17 Lord, I wear the helmet of salvation. Help me to. Thank you so very much for saving me, Lord. I get to spend eternity with you! What could possibly compare with that? Just as a physical helmet protects the head, I ask that your salvation protects my mind. You have "not given us the spirit of fear; but of power, and of love, and of a sound mind. (II Timothy 1:7) And as I "have the mind of Christ" (I Corinthians 2:16), help me to use it for your glory.

June 7

Deuteronomy 6; Job 37; Proverbs 14:34-35; Jeremiah 18:11-23; III John

Ephesians 6:18 Lord I pray in the spirit with all prayer and supplication. Help me to. Thank you so much for prayer. I get to talk with the king of Kings and lord of Lords! I get to talk with All Mighty God! And you delight to hear me. I am unworthy. Thank you for Jesus. Thank you that He made it possible for me to come to you in prayer. Teach me to pray, Lord.

June 8

Deuteronomy 7-8; Job 38; Proverbs 15:1-3; Jeremiah 19:1-7; Jude

Ephesians 6:14 Lord, I put on the breastplate of righteousness. Help me to. No matter what anyone says, no matter how often I fail, I wear your righteousness, because Jesus' blood has washed me of all my sin. I stand before you completely righteous, because of Jesus.

June 9

Deuteronomy 9-10; Job 39; Proverbs 15:4-5; Jeremiah 19:8-15; Revelation 1

Ephesians 6:14 Lord I put on the belt of truth. Help me to. You call yourself the truth. You call the enemy of our souls the father of lies. I choose truth. I will walk in truth, because you are truth. The truth is: you are God, I am not. You sent your son to save the world—and that includes me—out of love. Jesus paid for my sins on the cross. The truth is: You love me. And you have provided salvation for me. You have plans for me—good plans—not evil plans. You always provide for me. And you have work for me to do, telling others about you, making disciples. The truth is, because Jesus has washed my sins away, I get to spend eternity in your wonderful presence. In the light of all that, no matter what happens, I will stand firm and not be defeated.

June 10

Deuteronomy 11; Job 40; Proverbs 15:6-8; Jeremiah 20:1-9; Revelation 2

Ephesians 6:15 Lord, I wear the preparation of the Gospel of Peace. Help me to. Help me to recognize the opportunities you set before me to spread your Gospel of Peace. Help me to take courage and do it. Please give me creative ways to do this. Help me to see these souls as you see them. May I be prepared to tell them of the hope that lies in me. Help me to "study to show myself approved unto God, a workman that needeth not to be ashamed, rightly dividing the word of truth." (II Timothy 2:15) May I do all in my power to be prepared. And may you do all that isn't in my power to make me prepared with the Gospel of Peace.

June 11

Deuteronomy 12; Job 41; Proverbs 15:9-10; Jeremiah 20:10-18; Revelation 3

Ephesians 6:17 Lord, I take up the sword of the Spirit, which is your word. Help me to. Your word "is quick and powerful, and sharper than any two edged sword, piercing even to the dividing asunder of soul and spirit, and of the joints and marrow, and is a discerner of the thoughts and intents of the heart." (Hebrews 4:12). You've also said that your word will not return unto you "void, but it shall accomplish that which" you "please, and it shall prosper in the thing whereto" you "sent it." (Isaiah 55:11) May I use your word effectively, in a way that honors you, my Lord and my God.

June 12
Deuteronomy 13-14; Job 42; Proverbs 15:11-13; Jeremiah 21:1-7; Revelation 4
Ephesians 6:16 Lord, I take up the shield of faith, by which I may quench all the fiery darts of the wicked. Help me to. I know that "without faith it is impossible to please" you (Hebrews 11:6). Thank you for giving me faith in you. You are worthy of all faith. When the enemy of my soul tries to wound me, I turn to you in faith, knowing that you are God All Mighty, and he is not. You are in control. You have a plan. You will accomplish your plan. You are a good God. Your arm is not shortened. You will succeed in doing your will. The enemy of my soul will fail. I put my trust in You.

June 13
Deuteronomy 15-16; Psalm 120; Proverbs 15:14-15; Jeremiah 21:8-14; Revelation 5
Ephesians 6:17 Lord, I wear the helmet of salvation. Help me to. Thank you so very much for saving me, Lord. I get to spend eternity with you! What could possibly compare with that? Just as a physical helmet protects the head, I ask that your salvation protects my mind. You have "not given us the spirit of fear; but of power, and of love, and of a sound mind. (II Timothy 1:7) And as I "have the mind of Christ" (I Corinthians 2:16), help me to use it for your glory.

June 14
Deuteronomy 17-18; Psalm 121; Proverbs 15:16-18; Jeremiah 22:1-12; Revelation 6
Ephesians 6:18 Lord I pray in the spirit with all prayer and supplication. Help me to. Thank you so much for prayer. I get to talk with the king of Kings and lord of Lords! I get to talk with All Mighty God! And you delight to hear me. I am unworthy. Thank you for Jesus. Thank you that He made it possible for me to come to you in prayer. Teach me to pray, Lord.

June 15
Deuteronomy 19-20; Psalm 122; Proverbs 15:19-20; Jeremiah 22:13-30; Revelation 7
Ephesians 6:14 Lord, I put on the breastplate of righteousness. Help me to. No matter what anyone says, no matter how often I fail, I wear your righteousness, because Jesus' blood has washed me of all my sin. I stand before you completely righteous, because of Jesus.

June 16
Deuteronomy 21-22; Psalm 123; Proverbs 15:21-23; Jeremiah 23:1-20; Revelation 8
Ephesians 6:14 Lord I put on the belt of truth. Help me to. You call yourself the truth. You call the enemy of our souls the father of lies. I choose truth. I will walk in truth, because you are truth. The truth is: you are God, I am not. You sent your son to save the world—and that includes me—out of love. Jesus paid for my sins on the cross. The truth is: You love me. And you have provided salvation for me. You have plans for me—good plans—not evil plans. You always provide for me. And you have work for me to do, telling others about you, making disciples. The truth is, because Jesus has washed my sins away, I get to spend eternity in your wonderful presence. In the light of all that, no matter what happens, I will stand firm and not be defeated.

June 17

Deuteronomy 23; Psalm 124; Proverbs 15:24-25; Jeremiah 23:21-40; Revelation 9
Ephesians 6:15 Lord, I wear the preparation of the Gospel of Peace. Help me to. Help me to recognize the opportunities you set before me to spread your Gospel of Peace. Help me to take courage and do it. Please give me creative ways to do this. Help me to see these souls as you see them. May I be prepared to tell them of the hope that lies in me. Help me to "study to show myself approved unto God, a workman that needeth not to be ashamed, rightly dividing the word of truth." (II Timothy 2:15) May I do all in my power to be prepared. And may you do all that isn't in my power to make me prepared with the Gospel of Peace.

June 18
Deuteronomy 24; Psalm 125; Proverbs 15:26-28; Jeremiah 24; Revelation 10
Ephesians 6:17 Lord, I take up the sword of the Spirit, which is your word. Help me to. Your word "is quick and powerful, and sharper than any two edged sword, piercing even to the dividing asunder of soul and spirit, and of the joints and marrow, and is a discerner of the thoughts and intents of the heart." (Hebrews 4:12). You've also said that your word will not return unto you "void, but it shall accomplish that which" you "please, and it shall prosper in the thing whereto" you "sent it." (Isaiah 55:11) May I use your word effectively, in a way that honors you, my Lord and my God.

June 19
Deuteronomy 25; Psalm 126; Proverbs 15:29-30; Jeremiah 25:1-14; Revelation 11
Ephesians 6:16 Lord, I take up the shield of faith, by which I may quench all the fiery darts of the wicked. Help me to. I know that "without faith it is impossible to please" you (Hebrews 11:6). Thank you for giving me faith in you. You are worthy of all faith. When the enemy of my soul tries to wound me, I turn to you in faith, knowing that you are God All Mighty, and he is not. You are in control. You have a plan. You will accomplish your plan. You are a good God. Your arm is not shortened. You will succeed in doing your will. The enemy of my soul will fail. I put my trust in You.

June 20
Deuteronomy 26; Psalm 127; Proverbs 15:31-33; Jeremiah 25:15-38; Revelation 12
Ephesians 6:17 Lord, I wear the helmet of salvation. Help me to. Thank you so very much for saving me, Lord. I get to spend eternity with you! What could possibly compare with that? Just as a physical helmet protects the head, I ask that your salvation protects my mind. You have "not given us the spirit of fear; but of power, and of love, and of a sound mind. (II Timothy 1:7) And as I "have the mind of Christ" (I Corinthians 2:16), help me to use it for your glory.

June 21
Deuteronomy 27; Psalm 128; Proverbs 16:1-2; Jeremiah 26:1-9; Revelation 13
Ephesians 6:18 Lord I pray in the spirit with all prayer and supplication. Help me to. Thank you so much for prayer. I get to talk with the king of Kings and lord of Lords! I get to talk with All Mighty God! And you delight to hear me. I am unworthy. Thank you for Jesus. Thank you that He made it possible for me to come to you in prayer. Teach me to pray, Lord.

June 22
Deuteronomy 28; Psalm 129; Proverbs 16:3-5; Jeremiah 26:10-24; Revelation 14
Ephesians 6:14 Lord, I put on the breastplate of righteousness. Help me to. No matter what anyone says, no matter how often I fail, I wear your righteousness, because Jesus' blood has washed me of all my sin. I stand before you completely righteous, because of Jesus.

June 23

Deuteronomy 29; Psalm 130; Proverbs 16:6-7; Jeremiah 27:1-11; Revelation 15
Ephesians 6:14 Lord I put on the belt of truth. Help me to. You call yourself the truth. You call the enemy of our souls the father of lies. I choose truth. I will walk in truth, because you are truth. The truth is: you are God, I am not. You sent your son to save the world—and that includes me—out of love. Jesus paid for my sins on the cross. The truth is: You love me. And you have provided salvation for me. You have plans for me—good plans—not evil plans. You always provide for me. And you have work for me to do, telling others about you, making disciples. The truth is, because Jesus has washed my sins away, I get to spend eternity in your wonderful presence. In the light of all that, no matter what happens, I will stand firm and not be defeated.

June 24

Deuteronomy 30; Psalm 131; Proverbs 16:8-10; Jeremiah 27:12-22; Revelation 16
Ephesians 6:15 Lord, I wear the preparation of the Gospel of Peace. Help me to. Help me to recognize the opportunities you set before me to spread your Gospel of Peace. Help me to take courage and do it. Please give me creative ways to do this. Help me to see these souls as you see them. May I be prepared to tell them of the hope that lies in me. Help me to "study to show myself approved unto God, a workman that needeth not to be ashamed, rightly dividing the word of truth." (II Timothy 2:15) May I do all in my power to be prepared. And may you do all that isn't in my power to make me prepared with the Gospel of Peace.

June 25

Deuteronomy 31; Psalm 132; Proverbs 16:11-12; Jeremiah 28:1-9; Revelation 17
Ephesians 6:17 Lord, I take up the sword of the Spirit, which is your word. Help me to. Your word "is quick and powerful, and sharper than any two edged sword, piercing even to the dividing asunder of soul and spirit, and of the joints and marrow, and is a discerner of the thoughts and intents of the heart." (Hebrews 4:12). You've also said that your word will not return unto you "void, but it shall accomplish that which" you "please, and it shall prosper in the thing whereto" you "sent it." (Isaiah 55:11) May I use your word effectively, in a way that honors you, my Lord and my God.

June 26

Deuteronomy 32; Psalm 133; Proverbs 16:13-15; Jeremiah 28:10-17; Revelation 18
Ephesians 6:16
Lord, I take up the shield of faith, by which I may quench all the fiery darts of the wicked. Help me to. I know that "without faith it is impossible to please" you (Hebrews 11:6). Thank you for giving me faith in you. You are worthy of all faith. When the enemy of my soul tries to wound me, I turn to you in faith, knowing that you are God All Mighty, and he is not. You are in control. You have a plan. You will accomplish your plan. You are a good God. Your arm is not shortened. You will succeed in doing your will. The enemy of my soul will fail. I put my trust in You.

June 27

Deuteronomy 33; Psalm 134; Proverbs 16:16-17; Jeremiah 29:1-19; Revelation 19
Ephesians 6:17 Lord, I wear the helmet of salvation. Help me to. Thank you so very much for saving me, Lord. I get to spend eternity with you! What could possibly compare with that? Just as a physical helmet protects the head, I ask that your salvation protects my mind. You have "not given us the spirit of fear; but of power, and of love, and of a sound mind. (II Timothy 1:7) And as I "have the mind of Christ" (I Corinthians 2:16), help me to use it for your glory.

June 28

Deuteronomy 34; Psalm 135; Proverbs 16:18-20; Jeremiah 29:20-32; Revelation 20

Ephesians 6:18 Lord I pray in the spirit with all prayer and supplication. Help me to. Thank you so much for prayer. I get to talk with the king of Kings and lord of Lords! I get to talk with All Mighty God! And you delight to hear me. I am unworthy. Thank you for Jesus. Thank you that He made it possible for me to come to you in prayer. Teach me to pray, Lord.

June 29
Joshua 1-2; Psalm 136; Proverbs 16:21-22; Jeremiah 30:1-12; Revelation 21
Ephesians 6:13-18 Lord, I put on the whole armor of God. Please help me to. I put on the breastplate of righteousness, and the belt of truth. On my feet I wear the preparation of the Gospel of Peace. I take up the sword of the Spirit, which is the word of God, and the shield of faith, by which I may quench all the fiery darts of the wicked. I wear the helmet of salvation. I pray in the Spirit with all prayer and supplication. And having done all, I will stand.

June 30
Joshua 3-4; Psalm 137; Proverbs 16:23-25; Jeremiah 30:13-24; Revelation 22
"For the weapons of our warfare are not carnal, but mighty through God to the pulling down of strongholds; casting down imaginations, and every high thing that exalteth itself against the knowledge of God, and bringing into captivity every thought to the obedience o Christ." (I Corinthians 10:4-5) I "put on the armor of light" and "walk honestly, as in the day; not in rioting and drunkenness, not in chambering and wantonness, not in strife and envying." But I put "on the Lord Jesus Christ, and make not provision for the flesh, to fulfill the lusts thereof." (Romans 13:12-14)

July 1
Joshua 5-6; Psalm 138; Proverbs 16:26-27; Jeremiah 31:1-21; Matthew 1; Romans 1
Prayer for me to be a good wife/husband/family member to my spouse/family member.

July 2
Joshua 7-8; Psalm 139; Proverbs 16:28-30; Jeremiah 31:22-40; Matthew 2; Romans 2
Prayer for my spouse/family member to be a good wife/husband/family member to me. (Praying *for*, not *against*, my beloved one.)

July 3
Joshua 9; Psalm 140; Proverbs 16:31-33; Jeremiah 32:1-25; Matthew 3; Romans 3
Ephesians 3:16-19 Lord, I pray that you grant my beloved, according to the riches of your glory, to be strengthened with might by your Spirit in my beloved's inner man; That Christ may dwell in my beloved's heart by faith; that he/she being rooted and grounded in love, may be able to comprehend with all saints what is the breadth and length, and depth, and height; And to know the love of Christ, which passeth knowledge, that he/she might be filled with all the fullness of God.

July 4
Joshua 10; Psalm 141; Proverbs 17:1-2; Jeremiah 32:26-44; Matthew 4; Romans 4
Philippians 1:10-11 I pray that my beloved's love may abound in knowledge and all judgment—that he/she may test and assess all things according to excellence—that he/she may be sincere and not hypocritical and that he/she won't cause anyone to stumble—and that he/she will be filled with the fruits of righteousness.

July 5
Joshua 11-12; Psalm 142; Proverbs 17:3-5; Jeremiah 33:1-14; Matthew 5; Romans 5
"I will praise thee, O Lord, with my whole heart; I will show forth all of thy marvelous works. I will be glad and rejoice in thee: I will sing praise to thy name, O thou most high." (Psalm 9:1&2)

July 6

Joshua 13-14; Psalm 143; Proverbs 17:6-7; Jeremiah 33:15-26; Matthew 6; Romans 6
Hebrews 4:14-16 "Seeing then that we have a great high priest, that is passed into the Heavens, Jesus the Son of God, let us hold fast our profession. For we have not an high priest which cannot be touched with the feeling of our infirmities; but was in all points tempted like as we are, yet without sin. Let us therefore come boldly unto the throne of grace, that we may obtain mercy, and find grace to help in time of need."
July 7
Joshua 15; Psalm 144; Proverbs 17:8-10; Jeremiah 34:1-11; Matthew 7; Romans 7
Isaiah 65:24 "And it shall come to pass, that before they call, I will answer; and while they are yet speaking I will hear."
July 8
Joshua 16-17; Psalm 145; Proverbs 17:11-12; Jeremiah 34:12-22; Matthew 8; Romans 8
Prayer for me to be a good wife/husband/family member to my spouse/family member.
July 9
Joshua 18; Psalm 146; Proverbs 17:13-15; Jeremiah 35:1-11; Matthew 9; Romans 9
Prayer for my spouse/family member to be a good wife/husband/family member to me. (Praying *for*, not *against*, my beloved one.)
July 10
Joshua 19; Psalm 147; Proverbs 17:16-17; Jeremiah 35:12-19; Matthew 10; Romans 10
Ephesians 3:16-19 Lord, I pray that you grant my beloved, according to the riches of your glory, to be strengthened with might by your Spirit in my beloved's inner man; That Christ may dwell in my beloved's heart by faith; that he/she being rooted and grounded in love, may be able to comprehend with all saints what is the breadth and length, and depth, and height; And to know the love of Christ, which passeth knowledge, that he/she might be filled with all the fullness of God.
July 11
Joshua 20; Psalm 148; Proverbs 17:18-20; Jeremiah 36:1-19; Matthew 11; Romans 11
Philippians 1:10-11 I pray that my beloved's love may abound in knowledge and all judgment—that he/she may test and assess all things according to excellence—that he/she may be sincere and not hypocritical and that he/she won't cause anyone to stumble—and that he/she will be filled with the fruits of righteousness.
July 12
Joshua 21; Psalm 149; Proverbs 17:21-22; Jeremiah 36:20-32; Matthew 12; Romans 12
"I will praise thee, O Lord, with my whole heart; I will show forth all of they marvelous works. I will be glad and rejoice in thee: most high." (Psalm 9:1&2)
July 13
Joshua 22; Psalm 150; Proverbs 17:23-25; Jeremiah 37:1-10; Matthew 13; Romans 13
Hebrews 4:14-16"Seeing then that we have a great high priest, that is passed into the Heavens, Jesus the Son of God, let us hold fast our profession. For we have not an high priest which cannot be touched with the feeling of our infirmities; but was in all points tempted like as we are, yet without sin. Let us therefore come boldly unto the throne of grace, that we may obtain mercy, and find grace to help in time of need."
July 14
Joshua 23-24; Ecclesiastes 1; Proverbs 17:26-28; Jeremiah 37:11-21; Matthew 14; Romans 14

Isaiah 65:24 "And it shall come to pass, that before they call, I will answer; and while they are yet speaking I will hear."

July 15

Judges 1-2; Ecclesiastes 2; Proverbs 18:1-2; Jeremiah 38:1-13; Matthew 15; Romans 15

Prayer for me to be a good wife/husband/family member to my spouse/family member.

July 16

Judges 3-4; Ecclesiastes 3; Proverbs 18:3-4; Jeremiah 38:14-28; Matthew 16; Romans 16

Prayer for my spouse/family member to be a good wife/husband/family member to me. (Praying *for*, not *against*, my beloved one.)

July 17

Judges 5; Ecclesiastes 4; Proverbs 18:5-6; Jeremiah 39:1-10; Matthew 17; I Corinthians 1

Ephesians 3:16-19 Lord, I pray that you grant my beloved, according to the riches of your glory, to be strengthened with might by your Spirit in my beloved's inner man; That Christ may dwell in my beloved's heart by faith; that he/she being rooted and grounded in love, may be able to comprehend with all saints what is the breadth and length, and depth, and height; And to know the love of Christ, which passeth knowledge, that he/she might be filled with all the fullness of God.

July 18

Judges 6; Ecclesiastes 5; Proverbs 18:7-9; Jeremiah 39:11-18; Matthew 18; I Corinthians 2

Philippians 1:10-11 I pray that my beloved's love may abound in knowledge and all judgment—that he/she may test and assess all things according to excellence—that he/she may be sincere and not hypocritical and that he/she won't cause anyone to stumble—and that he/she will be filled with the fruits of righteousness.

July 19

Judges 7-8; Ecclesiastes 6; Proverbs 18:10-11; Jeremiah 40:1-8; Matthew 19; I Corinthians 3

"I will praise thee, O Lord, with my whole heart; I will show forth all of thy marvelous works. I will be glad and rejoice in thee: I will sing praise to thy name, O thou most high." (Psalm 9:1&2)

July 20

Judges 9; Ecclesiastes 7; Proverbs 18:12-14; Jeremiah 40:9-16; Matthew 20; I Corinthians 4

Hebrews 4:14-16 "Seeing then that we have a great high priest, that is passed into the Heavens, Jesus the Son of God, let us hold fast our profession. For we have not an high priest which cannot be touched with the feeling of our infirmities; but was in all points tempted like as we are, yet without sin. Let us therefore come boldly unto the throne of grace, that we may obtain mercy, and find grace to help in time of need."

July 21

Judges 10; Ecclesiastes 8; Proverbs 18:15-16; Jeremiah 41:1-10; Matthew 21; I Corinthians 5

Isaiah 65:24 "And it shall come to pass, that before they call, I will answer; and while they are yet speaking I will hear."

July 22

Judges 11; Ecclesiastes 9; Proverbs 18:17-18; Jeremiah 41:11-18; Matthew 22; I Corinthians 6

Prayer for me to be a good wife/husband/family member to my spouse/family member.
July 23
Judges 12-13; Ecclesiastes 10; Proverbs 18:20-21; Jeremiah 42:1-12; Matthew 23;
I Corinthians 7
Prayer for my spouse/family member to be a good wife/husband/family member to me.
(Praying *for*, not *against*, my beloved one.)
July 24
Judges 14-15; Ecclesiastes 11-12; Proverbs 18:22-24; Jeremiah 42:13-22; Matthew
24; I Corinthians 8
Ephesians 3:16-19 Lord, I pray that you grant my beloved, according to the riches of
your glory, to be strengthened with might by your Spirit in my beloved's inner man;
That Christ may dwell in my beloved's heart by faith; that he/she being rooted and
grounded in love, may be able to comprehend with all saints what is the breadth and
length, and depth, and height; And to know the love of Christ, which passeth
knowledge, that he/she might be filled with all the fullness of God.
July 25
Judges 16-17; Song of Solomon 1; Proverbs 19:1-2; Jeremiah 43:1-7; Matthew 25;
I Corinthians 9
Philippians 1:10-11 I pray that my beloved's love may abound in knowledge and all
judgment—that he/she may test and assess all things according to excellence—that
he/she may be sincere and not hypocritical and that he/she won't cause anyone to
stumble—and that he/she will be filled with the fruits of righteousness.
July 26
Judges 18; Song of Solomon 2; Proverbs 19:3-5; Jeremiah 43:8-13; Matthew 26;
I Corinthians 10
"I will praise thee, O Lord, with my whole heart; I will show forth all of thy marvelous
works. I will be glad and rejoice in thee: I will sing praise to thy name, O thou most
high." (Psalm 9:1&2)
July 27
Judges 19; Song of Solomon 3; Proverbs 19:6-7; Jeremiah 44:1-14; Matthew 27;
I Corinthians 11
Hebrews 4:14-16 "Seeing then that we have a great high priest, that is passed into the
Heavens, Jesus the Son of God, let us hold fast our profession. For we have not an
high priest which cannot be touched with the feeling of our infirmities; but was in all
points tempted like as we are, yet without sin. Let us therefore come boldly unto the
throne of grace, that we may obtain mercy, and find grace to help in time of need."
July 28
Judges 20; Song of Solomon 4; Proverbs 19:8-10; Jeremiah 44:15-30; Matthew 28
I Corinthians 12
Isaiah 65:24 "And it shall come to pass, that before they call, I will answer; and while
they are yet speaking I will hear."
July 29
Judges 21; Song of Solomon 5; Proverbs 19:11-12; Jeremiah 45; I Corinthians 13
Prayer for me to be a good wife/husband/family member to my spouse/family member.
July 30
Ruth 1-2; Song of Solomon 6; Proverbs 19:13-15; Jeremiah 46:1-12; I Corinthians 14
Prayer for my spouse/family member to be a good wife/husband/family member to me.
(Praying *for*, not *against*, my beloved one.)
July 31

Ruth 3-4; Song of Solomon 7; Proverbs 19:16-17; Jeremiah 46:13-28; I Corinthians 15
Ephesians 3:16-19 Lord, I pray that you grant my beloved, according to the riches of
your glory, to be strengthened with might by your Spirit in my beloved's inner man;
That Christ may dwell in my beloved's heart by faith; that he/she being rooted and
grounded in love, may be able to comprehend with all saints what is the breadth and
length, and depth, and height; And to know the love of Christ, which passeth
knowledge, that he/she might be filled with all the fullness of God.

August 1
I Samuel 1; Song of Solomon 8; Proverbs 19:18-20; Jeremiah 47; I Corinthians 16
(Proverbs 31:10-13) "Who can find a virtuous woman? for her price is far above rubies.
The heart of her husband doth safely trust in her, so that he shall have no need of
spoil. She will do him good and not evil all the days of her life. She seeketh wool, and
flax, and worketh willingly with her hands." May I do my beloved good all my life and
never evil. Help me to look for good things to do—servant things—and do them—
willingly. Help me to know that if I am virtuous, I am worthy of being looked for, pursued
by my beloved, and that I have value and am not a burden. Help me to be
trustworthy—in reality and also in my beloved's mind.

August 2
I Samuel 2; Psalm 1 ; Proverbs 19:21-22; Jeremiah 48:1-25; II Corinthians 1
(Proverbs 31:14) "She is like the merchants' ships; she bringeth her food from afar."
Lord, help me to bear the qualities of a merchant ship, carrying things of value—not a
garbage scow, which carried garbage. May all that I bring into conversation and all
things in life be of value, and not detrimental. May I be personally involved and not
expect another to do my part. May I not simply give orders, but bring in the things of
value myself. May I be willing and able to bring these things of value from a distance if
that's where they are.

August 3
I Samuel 3-4; Psalm 2; Proverbs 19:23-25; Jeremiah 48:26-47; II Corinthians 2
Five things to pray for my beloved
August 4
I Samuel 5-6; Psalm 3; Proverbs 19:26-27; Jeremiah 49:1-22; II Corinthians 3
Proverbs 31:15 "She riseth also while it is yet night, and giveth meat to her household,
and a portion to her maidens." Lord, help me to be the kind of person who is willing to
deprive myself in order that I may give. May I be willing to deny myself extra sleep
when someone needs me to give to him/her. I understand that I must rest—but this
proverbs 31 woman, after resting her body and mind and soul, got up at the point of
having rested enough and denied herself the luxury of resting abundantly, because
others had a need for her to get busy and give. May I be this way—resting according to
wisdom, but not according to greed. And may I give this way too—according to wisdom
and love, not according to greed and self-centeredness.

August 5
I Samuel 7-8; Psalm 4; Proverbs 19:28-29; Jeremiah 49:23-39; II Corinthians 4
Proverbs 31:16 "She considereth a field, and buyeth it: with the fruit of her hands she
planteth a vineyard." Help me Lord to give thought and consideration as to what you
want me to do, and then put wings to my prayers and thoughts and consideration and
do what is in my power to make it happen. And then when it happens, help me to be
busy about the work. The proverbs 31 woman thought about it, then bought it, then
began using it. It was aimed at fruit-bearing—in her case: grapes. May I aim for fruit-
bearing. It may not be a physical piece of land and vineyard, but please open my eyes

and means to considering and buying and planting whatever "piece of land" You desire for me to.

August 6
I Samuel 9; Psalm 5; Proverbs 20:1-3; Jeremiah 50:1-20; II Corinthians 5
Five things to pray for my beloved

August 7
I Samuel 10; Psalm 6; Proverbs 20:4-5; Jeremiah 50:21-46; II Corinthians 6
Proverbs 31:17 "She girdeth her loins with strength, and strengtheneth her arms." Help me Lord, to put on strength and so *be* strength. If I don't do what I can, which is to put strength on—to latch hold of it and make it part of me—how can I expect to be strong? Help me to cover myself with strength, especially those parts of me that no one else sees. If I strengthen those secret parts of me and my life, those parts of me and my life that others see will also be strengthened. Help me, Lord—make me to be strong, both in secret and in public.

August 8
I Samuel 11-12; Psalm 7; Proverbs 20:6-8; Jeremiah 51:1-19; II Corinthians 7
Proverbs 31:18 "She perceiveth that her merchandise is good: her candle goeth not out by night." Lord, help me to perceive correctly and be perceived correctly. I need not worry that the truth shines forth when I have given my best—when I have labored as I should, not being lazy. Then I know that what I have to contribute is good, for I have done my best. So Lord, help me to labor for you, giving you my best—faithfully—even when it costs me.

August 9
I Samuel 13; Psalm 8; Proverbs 20:9-10; Jeremiah 51:20-40; II Corinthians 8
Five things to pray for my beloved

August 10
I Samuel 14; Psalm 9; Proverbs 20:11-13; Jeremiah 51:41-64; II Corinthians 9
Proverbs 31:19 "She layeth her hands to the spindle, and her hands hold the distaff." Lord help me to begin and then to continue on in whatever you call me to do. May I be willing to get personally involved—laying my hands on this work—touching it myself—pressing into it in commitment as I hold it and so make it mine—my work for Your glory, which is really Yours entrusted to me. May I do what You set before me to do.

August 11
I Samuel 15-16; Psalm 10; Proverbs 20:14-15; Jeremiah 52:1-15; II Corinthians 10
Proverbs 31:20 "She stretcheth out her hand to the poor; yea, she reacheth forth her hands to the needy." Help me Lord, to live a life that is purposely reaching out to those in need—personally reaching out—not *only* writing a check for those who reach out, but in addition to writing a check, to do this *myself* also. Help me to touch—that personal involvement—the poor and the needy. Help me to see who are poor and who are needy and not just assume that I know already. Some have needs that go beyond money. Some are poor even though they have thousands in the bank. Help me to reach out to them.

August 12
I Samuel 17; Psalm 11; Proverbs 20:16-18; Jeremiah 52:16-34; II Corinthians 11
Five things to pray for my beloved

August 13
I Samuel 18; Psalm 12; Proverbs 20:19-20; Lamentations 1:1-11; II Corinthians 12
Proverbs 31:21 "She is not afraid of the snow for her household: for all her household are clothed with scarlet." Lord, help me to live my life in such a way that I will have no

reason to fear for my household, no matter what comes. As much as depends on me, may I be faithful to do it, and leave the rest in Your hands, that I be not afraid for my household, knowing that I have done my part, and that You will do Yours. Thank You Lord.

August 14
I Samuel 19; Psalm 13; Proverbs 20:20-22; Lamentations 1:12-22; II Corinthians 13
Proverbs 31:22 "She maketh herself coverings of tapestry; her clothing is silk and purple." Help me, Lord, to make things with my own hands and give it my best. This proverbs 31 woman made clothing for herself and it was the best. It was silk and the sought-after, valuable "purple". Help me to remember that it's alright if I have something of value and that it's alright to spend time on making something for me. Help me not to confuse a servant's heart with thinking I'm of no value. You gave Your Son for me, showing me that You find me valuable. Thank You Lord.

August 15
I Samuel 20; Psalm 14; Proverbs 20:23-24; Lamentations 2:1-10; Mark 1
Five things to pray for my beloved

August 16
I Samuel 21-22; Psalm 15; Proverbs 20:25-27; Lamentations 2:11-22; Mark 2
Proverbs 31:23 "Her husband is known in the gates, when he sitteth among the elders of the land." Lord may my life be lived in such a way that I not only bring glory to You, but also to my beloved, especially when he/she is out and about in the public eye. May he/she be known in a good and positive way, among those who have wisdom and authority. And may I have a hand in this, doing all in my power to promote him/her—ultimately for Your honor and glory, but also for my beloved's.

August 17
I Samuel 23-24; Psalm 16; Proverbs 20:28-30; Lamentations 3:1-21; Mark 3
Proverbs 31:24 "She maketh fine linen, and selleth it; and delivereth girdles unto the merchant." Lord, help me to make whatever You've given me the talent and means of making. And may I do it for Your glory. But may I not stop there, but take it to the next step and sell it—whether literally or figuratively—receiving from the blessings You mean for me to have from it. And may I use these blessings the way You intend. And finally, help me to deliver to others whatever it is You've given me the ability to do and make, that the blessings will not stop, but will be passed along. Help me to give You my best.

August 18
I Samuel 25; Psalm 17; Proverbs 21:1-2; Lamentations 3:22-41; Mark 4
Five things to pray for my beloved

August 19
I Samuel 26-27; Psalm18; Proverbs 21:3-5; Lamentations 3:42-66; Mark 5; Galatians 1
Proverbs 31:25 "Strength and honour are her clothing; and she shall rejoice in time to come." Lord, help me to be the person You created me to be. May I be a person of strength and honor. May my strength and honor cover me like clothing covers my body—touching all of me—covering what is private, but not taking it away—enhancing what is public, giving it beauty and grace and an artistic look. May my strength and honor be in You. The joy of the Lord is my strength (Nehemiah 8:10). And being clothed in strength and honor, may I rejoice. Even if today is hard, help me to remember that I will rejoice in time to come—for "weeping may endure for a night, but joy cometh in the morning." (Psalm 30:5)

August 20

I Samuel 28-29; Psalm 19; Proverbs 21:6-7; Lamentations 4:1-12; Mark 6; Galatians 2
Proverbs 31:26 "She openeth her mouth with wisdom; and in her tongue is the law of kindness." Lord, may I have a kind tongue and use it wisely. May I remember to use it and not stay silent all the time. But in using it, may I use wisdom and kindness—both of which know that there is a right timing and a right choice of words and tone of voice that when all combined together make for wise and kind speech. Help me so to speak.

August 21
I Samuel 30-31; Psalm 20; Proverbs 21:8-10; Lamentations 4:13-22; Mark 7; Galatians 3

Five things to pray for my beloved
August 22
II Samuel 1; Psalm 21; Proverbs 21:11-12; Lamentations 5:1-11; Mark 8; Galatians 4
Proverbs 31:27 "She looketh well to the ways of her household, and eateth not the bread of idleness." Lord, help me to be observant where my household is concerned. Help me to purposefully look and notice everything that concerns my household. And may I not stop with the looking and observing, but may I act upon what I observe and not be idle. May I not allow things to slip by. But may I do what needs to be done, even when I don't feel like it for one reason or another. Help me not to cultivate idleness.

August 23
II Samuel 2; Psalm 22; Proverbs 21:13-15; Lamentations 5:12-22; Mark 9; Galatians 5
Proverbs 31:28 "Her children arise up, and call her blessed; her husband also, and he praiseth her." Whether children of my body or children of my ministry, or children of my heart, whether they are near or far, teach me how to pray in regard to them. Lord may I live every day in such a way as being deserving of having the children rise up and call me blessed.

August 24
II Samuel 3; Psalm 23; Proverbs 21:16-17; Ezekiel 1; Mark 10; Galatians 6
Five things to pray for my beloved
August 25
II Samuel 4-5; Psalm 24; Proverbs 21:18-20; Ezekiel 2; Mark 11; Ephesians 1
Proverbs 31:28 "Her children arise up, and call her blessed; her husband also, and he praiseth her." May I *be* all that I am supposed to be, so as to be deserving of my beloved's praise and the children's blessings—whether or not they give it to me. Please help me to live so closely to You that I will be deserving of their blessings and praises, but not worry about whether or not they give it to me. May I leave that to be between You and them. And may I be willing to give my beloved and my parents praise and blessings.

August 26
II Samuel 6; Psalm 25; Proverbs 21:21-22; Ezekiel 3; Mark 12; Ephesians 2
Proverbs 31:29 "Many daughters have done virtuously, but thou excellest them all." Lord, when all is said and done, all that is going to matter is You and how we lived virtuously. May I live my life virtuously for You. May I do such a good job at it, that when compared to others, I will excel them all—not so that I can be number one—but that my aim will be to be as virtuous as You created me to be—and that all of us will so strive. May I succeed, Lord. May I not see myself as a failure and as less, but as one who is virtuous—And this is the place of excelling them all: in virtue. May I never forget the value of virtue.

August 27
II Samuel 7; Psalm 26; Proverbs 21:23-25; Ezekiel 4; Mark 13; Ephesians 3

Five things to pray for my beloved
August 28
II Samuel 8-9; Psalm 27; Proverbs 21:26-27; Ezekiel 5; Mark 14:1-42; Ephesians 4
Proverbs 31:30 "Favour is deceitful, and beauty is vain: but a woman that feareth the LORD, she shall be praised." Lord, help me to discern between what is real and what is empty. May I not concentrate on illusions like favor and beauty. At best, these are only momentary. But instead, may I spend my life and all that I am and have in fearing You—holding You in awesome esteem, for You are my God. And may I allow this very thing to be my praise.

August 29
II Samuel 10-11; Psalm 28; Proverbs 21:28-29; Ezekiel 6; Mark 14:43-72; Ephesians 5
Proverbs 31:31 "Give her of the fruit of her hands; and let her own works praise her in the gates." Lord, please give me fruit. You've promised that the righteous will still bear fruit in old age (Psalm 92:14). This is my heart's desire—that I will never stop bearing fruit unto You until you call me home. May this fruit be my praise—not *me* but my *fruit*. May my fruit take me to the places of influence, wherever You would have me to go.

August 30
II Samuel 12; Psalm 29; Proverbs 21:30-31; Ezekiel 7; Mark 15:1-14; Ephesians 6
Five things to pray for my beloved
August 31
II Samuel 13; Psalm 30; Proverbs 22:1-3; Ezekiel 8; Mark 15:15-47
Five things to pray for my beloved
September 1
II Samuel 14; Psalm 31; Proverbs 22:4-5; Ezekiel 9; Mark 16:1-8
Lord, may my love suffer long. (I Corinthian 13:4)
[The Greek word for charity means love]
When I am injured, may my love not lose heart, but bravely persevere and endure the troubles. May the thought of punishing or taking vengeance upon my beloved not even enter my mind. May my love take heart, even if times grow hard—even if my beloved offends me. Lord I put on mercy. (Colossians 3:12)

September 2
II Samuel 15; Psalm 32; Proverbs 22:6-8; Ezekiel 10; Mark 16:9-20; Philippians 1
Lord, may my love be kind. (I Corinthians 13:14) May it show itself by mildness and kindness. May it show itself by usefulness, goodness, and pleasantness. May my love be virtuous. Lord, I put on kindness. (Colossians 3:12)

September 3
II Samuel 16; Psalm 33; Proverbs 22:9-11; Ezekiel 11; Philippians 2
Lord, may my love not envy. (I Corinthians 13:4) May my love not seek to possess what rightfully belongs to my beloved. May it not strive against my beloved, nor be jealous in the sense of wanting to deprive my beloved of any rightful, good thing or person or place. May my love cheer on my beloved in all righteousness, desiring for my beloved to be all that you purpose. Lord, I put on humbleness. (Colossians 3:12)

September 4
II Samuel 17; Psalm 34; Proverbs 22:12-14; Ezekiel 12; Philippians 3
Lord, may my love not vaunt itself. (I Corinthians 13:4) May it not set out to display me. May my love not be boastful of myself, but rather may my love seek to display my beloved and boast of him. Lord, I put on meekness. (Colossians 3:12)

September 5
II Samuel 18; Psalm 35; Proverbs 22:15-16; Ezekiel 13; Philippians 4

Lord, may my love not be puffed up. (I Corinthians 13:4) May it not be self-inflating and prideful. May it not be a snobby kind of love, but rather, a humble kind—the kind of love that wants my beloved to be seen as the hero of the story instead of me. Lord, I put on longsuffering. (Colossians 3:12)

September 6
II Samuel 19; Psalm 36; Proverbs 22:17-18; Ezekiel 14; Colossians 1
Lord, may my love not behave itself unseemly. (I Corinthians 13:5) May it not conduct itself dishonorably, bringing shame to my beloved. May it not be indecent or disgraceful, but rather, full of grace, honour and decency. Lord, I put on forbearance. (Colossians 3:13)

September 7
II Samuel 20; Psalm 37; Proverbs 22:19-21; Ezekiel 15; Colossians 2
Lord, may my love not seek her own. (I Corinthians 13:5) May it not meditate on me. May my love not make self-centered demands or be aimed at me, but rather may my love seek for the good of my beloved, craving for what is best for my beloved and be "beloved-centered" rather than "self-centered". Lord, I put on forgiveness. (Colossians 3:13)

September 8
II Samuel 21; Psalm 38; Proverbs 22:22-23; Ezekiel 16:1-34; Colossians 3
Lord, may my love not be easily provoked. (I Corinthians 13:5) May it not be easily angered or exasperated. May it not be easily irritated or become sharp. But rather, may it bravely persevere and be kind. Lord, above all, I put on love. (Colossians 3:14)

September 9
II Samuel 22; Psalm 39; Proverbs 22:24-25; Ezekiel 16:35-63; Colossians 4
Lord, may my love think no evil. (I Corinthians 13:5) May it not set itself up as a judge against my beloved, judging the bad—but rather, may my love think on the good. When a destructive thought comes, let me immediately think on something constructive, taking inventory on constructive things, which build up rather than tear down. Lord, I put on mercy. (Colossians 3:12)

September 10
II Samuel 23; Psalm 40; Proverbs 22:26-27; Ezekiel 17; I Thessalonians 1
Lord, may my love not rejoice in iniquity. (I Corinthians 13:6) May it not be glad and thrive over wrongfulness in my beloved. May my love not be full of cheer over injustice or unrighteousness—neither my beloved's nor my own. Lord I put on kindness. (Colossians 3: 12)

September 11
II Samuel 24; Psalm 41; Proverbs 22:28-29; Ezekiel 18; I Thessalonians 2
Lord, may my love rejoice in the truth (I Corinthians 13:6) May it be such a joyous love, that I treat the truth as though it were such a glad thing, that it actually deserves congratulations and I join in on rejoicing. As you, Lord, mingle mercy with truth (Psalm 57:10), when the truth in my beloved is painful to me, may I give my beloved mercy. In this way I can rejoice even in hard truths, for they offer me opportunities to demonstrate mercy and to show love. Lord I put on humbleness. (Colossians 3:12)

September 12
I Kings 1; Psalm 42-43; Proverbs 23:1-3; Ezekiel 19; I Thessalonians 3
Lord, may my love bear all things (I Corinthians 13:7) May it protect my beloved like a roof that covers my beloved's faults, hiding them from all that threatens my beloved. Lord I put on meekness. (Colossians 3:12)

September 13

I Kings 2; Psalm 44; Proverbs 23:4-5; Ezekiel 20; I Thessalonians 4

Lord, may my love believe all things (I Corinthians 13:7) May it be one that has faith in my beloved, choosing to believe my beloved and believe in my beloved, entrusting my beloved with my love and committing to love my beloved. Lord I put on longsuffering. (Colossians 3:12)

September 14

I Kings 3-4; Psalm 45; Proverbs 23:6-8; Ezekiel 21; I Thessalonians 5

Lord, may my love hope all things (I Corinthians 13:7) May it be the kind that trusts. May my love be so desirous of a good outcome that it expects it to happen, so much so that it confides in my loved one—it hopes all things. Lord I put on forbearance. (Colossians 3:13)

September 15

I Kings 5-6; Psalm 46; Proverbs 23:9-11; Ezekiel 22; II Thessalonians 1

Lord, may my love endure all things. (I Corinthians 13:7) May it remain no matter what. And if need be that it suffer, may my love be the kind that suffers bravely and calmly and not flee away, but perseveres and takes whatever comes patiently and calmly. May my love be the staying-under sort—the sort that holds up my beloved like a supporting wall holds up the roof. May it endure. Lord I put on forgiveness. (Colossians 3:13)

September 16

I Kings 7; Psalm 47; Proverbs 23:12-14; Ezekiel 23; II Thessalonians 2

Lord, may my love suffer long. (I Corinthian 13:4) When I am injured, may my love not lose heart, but bravely persevere and endure the troubles. May the thought of punishing or taking vengeance upon my beloved not even enter my mind. May my love take heart, even if times grow hard—even if my beloved offends me. Lord I put on mercy. (Colossians 3:12)

September 17

I Kings 8; Psalm 48; Proverbs 23:15-16; Ezekiel 24; II Thessalonians 3

Lord, may my love be kind. (I Corinthians 13:14) May it show itself by mildness and kindness. May it show itself by usefulness, goodness, and pleasantness. May my love be virtuous. Lord, I put on kindness. (Colossians 3:12)

September 18

I Kings 9-10; Psalm 49; Proverbs 23:17-18; Ezekiel 25; I Timothy 1

Lord, may my love not envy. (I Corinthians 13:4) May my love not seek to possess what rightfully belongs to my beloved. May it not strive against my beloved, nor be jealous in the sense of wanting to deprive my beloved of any rightful, good thing or person or place. May my love cheer on my beloved in all righteousness, desiring for my beloved to be all that you purpose. Lord, I put on humbleness. (Colossians 3:12)

September 19

I Kings 11; Psalm 50; Proverbs 23:19-21; Ezekiel 26; I Timothy 2

Lord, may my love not vaunt itself.(I Corinthians 13:4) May it not set out to display me. May my love not be boastful of myself, but rather may my love seek to display my beloved and boast of him/her. Lord, I put on meekness. (Colossians 3:12)

September 20

I Kings 12; Psalm 51; Proverbs 23:22-23; Ezekiel 27; I Timothy 3

Lord, may my love not be puffed up. (I Corinthians 13:4) May it not be self-inflating and prideful. May it not be a snobby kind of love, but rather, a humble kind—the kind of love that wants my beloved to be seen as the hero of the story instead of me. Lord, I put on longsuffering. (Colossians 3:12)

September 21
I Kings 13; Psalm 52; Proverbs 23:24-26; Ezekiel 28; I Timothy 4

Lord, may my love not behave itself unseemly. (I Corinthians 13:5) May it not conduct itself dishonorably, bringing shame to my beloved. May it not be indecent or disgraceful, but rather, full of grace, honour and decency. Lord, I put on forbearance. (Colossians 3:13)

September 22
I Kings 14; Psalm 53; Proverbs 23:27-28; Ezekiel 29; I Timothy 5

Lord, may my love not seek her own. (I Corinthians 13:5) May it not meditate on me. May my love not make self-centered demands or be aimed at me, but rather may my love seek for the good of my beloved, craving for what is best for my beloved and be "beloved-centered" rather than "self-centered". Lord, I put on forgiveness. (Colossians 3:13)

September 23
I Kings 15; Psalm 54; Proverbs 23:29-30; Ezekiel 30; I Timothy 6

Lord, may my love not be easily provoked. (I Corinthians 13:5) May it not be easily angered or exasperated. May it not be easily irritated or become sharp. But rather, may it bravely persevere and be kind. Lord, above all, I put on love. (Colossians 3:14)

September 24
I Kings 16; Psalm 55; Proverbs 23:31-33; Ezekiel 31; II Timothy 1

Lord, may my love think no evil. (I Corinthians 13:5) May it not set itself up as a judge against my beloved, judging the bad—but rather, may my love think on the good. When a destructive thought comes, let me immediately think on something constructive, taking inventory on constructive things, which build up rather than tear down. Lord, I put on mercy. (Colossians 3:12)

September 25
I Kings 17; Psalm 56; Proverbs 23:34-35; Ezekiel 32; II Timothy 2

Lord, may my love not rejoice in iniquity. (I Corinthians 13:6) May it not be glad and thrive over wrongfulness in my beloved. May my love not be full of cheer over injustice or unrighteousness—neither my beloved's nor my own. Lord I put on kindness. (Colossians 3: 12)

September 26
I Kings 18; Psalm 57; Proverbs 24:1-2; Ezekiel 33; II Timothy 3

Lord, may my love rejoice in the truth (I Corinthians 13:6) May it be such a joyous love, that I treat the truth as though it were such a glad thing, that it actually deserves congratulations and I join in on rejoicing. As you, Lord, mingle mercy with truth (Psalm 57:10), when the truth in my beloved is painful to me, may I give my beloved mercy. In this way I can rejoice even in hard truths, for they offer me opportunities to demonstrate mercy and to show love. Lord I put on humbleness. (Colossians 3:12)

September 27
I Kings 19; Psalm 58; Proverbs 24:3-4; Ezekiel 34; II Timothy 4

Lord, may my love bear all things. (I Corinthians 13:7) May it protect my beloved like a roof that covers my beloved's faults, hiding them from all that threatens my beloved. Lord I put on meekness. (Colossians 3:12)

September 28
I Kings 20; Psalm 59; Proverbs 24:5-7; Ezekiel 35; Titus 1

Lord, may my love believe all things (I Corinthians 13:7) May it be one that has faith in my beloved, choosing to believe my beloved and believe in my beloved, entrusting my beloved with my love and committing to love my beloved. Lord I put on longsuffering. (Colossians 3:12)

September 29

I Kings 21; Psalm 60; Proverbs 24:8-10; Ezekiel 36; Titus 2

Lord, may my love hope all things (I Corinthians 13:7) May it be the kind that trusts. May my love be so desirous of a good outcome that it expects it to happen, so much so that it confides in my loved one—it hopes all things. Lord I put on forbearance. (Colossians 3:13)

September 30

I Kings 22; Psalm 61; Proverbs 24:11-12; Ezekiel 37; Titus 3

Lord, may my love endure all things. (I Corinthians 13:7) May it remain no matter what. And if need be that it suffer, may my love be the kind that suffers bravely and calmly and not flee away, but perseveres and takes whatever comes patiently and calmly. May my love be the staying-under sort—the sort that holds up my beloved like a supporting wall holds up the roof. May it endure. Lord I put on forgiveness. (Colossians 3:13)

October 1

II Kings 1-2; Psalm 62; Proverbs 24:13-14; Ezekiel 28; Philemon

Ephesians 6:14 Lord, I put on the breastplate of righteousness. Help me to. No matter what anyone says, no matter how often I fail, I wear your righteousness, because Jesus' blood has washed me of all my sin. I stand before you completely righteous, because of Jesus

October 2

II Kings 3; Psalm 63; Proverbs 24:15-18; Ezekiel 39; Luke 1

Ephesians 6:14 Lord I put on the belt of truth. Help me to. You call yourself the truth. You call the enemy of our souls the father of lies. I choose truth. I will walk in truth, because you are truth. The truth is: you are God, I am not. You sent your son to save the world—and that includes me—out of love. Jesus paid for my sins on the cross. The truth is: You love me. And you have provided salvation for me. You have plans for me—good plans—not evil plans. You always provide for me. And you have work for me to do, telling others about you, making disciples. The truth is, because Jesus has washed my sins away, I get to spend eternity in your wonderful presence. In the light of all that, no matter what happens, I will stand firm and not be defeated.

October 3

II Kings 4; Psalm 64; Proverbs 24:19-20; Ezekiel 40:1-23; Luke 2

Ephesians 6:15 Lord, I wear the preparation of the Gospel of Peace. Help me to. Help me to recognize the opportunities you set before me to spread your Gospel of Peace. Help me to take courage and do it. Please give me creative ways to do this. Help me to see these souls as you see them. May I be prepared to tell them of the hope that lies in me. Help me to "study to show myself approved unto God, a workman that needeth not to be ashamed, rightly dividing the word of truth." (II Timothy 2:15) May I do all in my power to be prepared. And may you do all that isn't in my power to make me prepared with the Gospel of Peace.

October 4

II Kings 5-6; Psalm 65; Proverbs 24:21-22; Ezekiel 40:24-49; Luke 3

Ephesians 6:17 Lord, I take up the sword of the Spirit, which is your word. Help me to. Your word "is quick and powerful, and sharper than any two edged sword, piercing even to the dividing asunder of soul and spirit, and of the joints and marrow, and is a discerner of the thoughts and intents of the heart." (Hebrews 4:12). You've also said that your word will not return unto you "void, but it shall accomplish that which" you "please, and it shall prosper in the thing whereto" you "sent it." (Isaiah 55:11) May I use your word effectively, in a way that honors you, my Lord and my God.

October 5
II Kings 7-8; Psalm 66; Proverbs 24:23-26; Ezekiel 41; Luke 4; Acts 1
Ephesians 6:16 Lord, I take up the shield of faith, by which I may quench all the fiery darts of the wicked. Help me to. I know that "without faith it is impossible to please" you (Hebrews 11:6). Thank you for giving me faith in you. You are worthy of all faith. When the enemy of my soul tries to wound me, I turn to you in faith, knowing that you are God All Mighty, and he is not. You are in control. You have a plan. You will accomplish your plan. You are a good God. Your arm is not shortened. You will succeed in doing your will. The enemy of my soul will fail. I put my trust in You.

October 6
II Kings 9; Psalm 67; Proverbs 24:27; Ezekiel 42; Luke 5; Acts 2
Ephesians 6:17 Lord, I wear the helmet of salvation. Help me to. Thank you so very much for saving me, Lord. I get to spend eternity with you! What could possibly compare with that? Just as a physical helmet protects the head, I ask that your salvation protects my mind. You have "not given us the spirit of fear; but of power, and of love, and of a sound mind. (II Timothy 1:7) And as I "have the mind of Christ" (I Corinthians 2:16), help me to use it for your glory.

October 7
II Kings 10; Psalm 68; Proverbs 24:28-29; Ezekiel 43; Luke 6; Acts 3
Ephesians 6:18 Lord I pray in the spirit with all prayer and supplication. Help me to. Thank you so much for prayer. I get to talk with the king of Kings and lord of Lords! I get to talk with All Mighty God! And you delight to hear me. I am unworthy. Thank you for Jesus. Thank you that He made it possible for me to come to you in prayer. Teach me to pray, Lord.

October 8
II Kings 11; Psalm 69; Proverbs 24:30-34; Ezekiel 44; Luke 7; Acts 4
Ephesians 6:14 Lord, I put on the breastplate of righteousness. Help me to. No matter what anyone says, no matter how often I fail, I wear your righteousness, because Jesus' blood has washed me of all my sin. I stand before you completely righteous, because of Jesus.

October 9
II Kings 12-13; Psalm 70; Proverbs 25:1-2; Ezekiel 45; Luke 8; Acts 5
Ephesians 6:14 Lord I put on the belt of truth. Help me to. You call yourself the truth. You call the enemy of our souls the father of lies. I choose truth. I will walk in truth, because you are truth. The truth is: you are God, I am not. You sent your son to save the world—and that includes me—out of love. Jesus paid for my sins on the cross. The truth is: You love me. And you have provided salvation for me. You have plans for me—good plans—not evil plans. You always provide for me. And you have work for me to do, telling others about you, making disciples. The truth is, because Jesus has washed my sins away, I get to spend eternity in your wonderful presence. In the light of all that, no matter what happens, I will stand firm and not be defeated.

October 10
II Kings 14; Psalm 71; Proverbs 25:3; Ezekiel 46; Luke 9; Acts 6
Ephesians 6:15 Lord, I wear the preparation of the Gospel of Peace. Help me to. Help me to recognize the opportunities you set before me to spread your Gospel of Peace. Help me to take courage and do it. Please give me creative ways to do this. Help me to

see these souls as you see them. May I be prepared to tell them of the hope that lies in me. Help me to "study to show myself approved unto God, a workman that needeth not to be ashamed, rightly dividing the word of truth." (II Timothy 2:15) May I do all in my power to be prepared. And may you do all that isn't in my power to make me prepared with the Gospel of Peace.

October 11
II Kings 15; Psalm 72; Proverbs 25:4-5; Ezekiel 47; Luke 10; Acts 7

Ephesians 6:17 Lord, I take up the sword of the Spirit, which is your word. Help me to. Your word "is quick and powerful, and sharper than any two edged sword, piercing even to the dividing asunder of soul and spirit, and of the joints and marrow, and is a discerner of the thoughts and intents of the heart." (Hebrews 4:12). You've also said that your word will not return unto you "void, but it shall accomplish that which" you "please, and it shall prosper in the thing whereto" you "sent it." (Isaiah 55:11) May I use your word effectively, in a way that honors you, my Lord and my God.

October 12
II Kings 16; Psalm 73; Proverbs 25:6-8; Ezekiel 48; Luke 11; Acts 8

Ephesians 6:16 Lord, I take up the shield of faith, by which I may quench all the fiery darts of the wicked. Help me to. I know that "without faith it is impossible to please" you (Hebrews 11:6). Thank you for giving me faith in you. You are worthy of all faith. When the enemy of my soul tries to wound me, I turn to you in faith, knowing that you are God All Mighty, and he is not. You are in control. You have a plan. You will accomplish your plan. You are a good God. Your arm is not shortened. You will succeed in doing your will. The enemy of my soul will fail. I put my trust in You.

October 13
II Kings 17; Psalm 74; Proverbs 25:9-10; Daniel 1; Luke 12; Acts 9

Ephesians 6:17 Lord, I wear the helmet of salvation. Help me to. Thank you so very much for saving me, Lord. I get to spend eternity with you! What could possibly compare with that? Just as a physical helmet protects the head, I ask that your salvation protects my mind. You have "not given us the spirit of fear; but of power, and of love, and of a sound mind. (II Timothy 1:7) And as I "have the mind of Christ" (I Corinthians 2:16), help me to use it for your glory.

October 14
II Kings 18; Psalm 75; Proverbs 25:11-13; Daniel 2; Luke 13; Acts 10

Ephesians 6:18 Lord I pray in the spirit with all prayer and supplication. Help me to. Thank you so much for prayer. I get to talk with the king of Kings and lord of Lords! I get to talk with All Mighty God! And you delight to hear me. I am unworthy. Thank you for Jesus. Thank you that He made it possible for me to come to you in prayer. Teach me to pray, Lord.

October 15
II Kings 19; Psalm 76; Proverbs 25:14-15; Daniel 3; Luke 14; Acts 11

Ephesians 6:14 Lord, I put on the breastplate of righteousness. Help me to. No matter what anyone says, no matter how often I fail, I wear your righteousness, because Jesus' blood has washed me of all my sin. I stand before you completely righteous, because of Jesus.

October 16
II Kings 20-21; Psalm 77; Proverbs 25:16-18; Daniel 4; Luke 15; Acts 12

Ephesians 6:14 Lord I put on the belt of truth. Help me to. You call yourself the truth. You call the enemy of our souls the father of lies. I choose truth. I will walk in truth, because you are truth. The truth is: you are God, I am not. You sent your son to save the world—and that includes me—out of love. Jesus paid for my sins on the cross. The truth is: You love me. And you have provided salvation for me. You have plans for me—good plans—not evil plans. You always provide for me. And you have work for me to do, telling others about you, making disciples. The truth is, because Jesus has washed my sins away, I get to spend eternity in your wonderful presence. In the light of all that, no matter what happens, I will stand firm and not be defeated.

October 17
II Kings 22; Psalm 78; Proverbs 25:19-20; Daniel 5; Luke 16; Acts 13
Ephesians 6:15 Lord, I wear the preparation of the Gospel of Peace. Help me to. Help me to recognize the opportunities you set before me to spread your Gospel of Peace. Help me to take courage and do it. Please give me creative ways to do this. Help me to see these souls as you see them. May I be prepared to tell them of the hope that lies in me. Help me to "study to show myself approved unto God, a workman that needeth not to be ashamed, rightly dividing the word of truth." (II Timothy 2:15) May I do all in my power to be prepared. And may you do all that isn't in my power to make me prepared with the Gospel of Peace.

October 18
II Kings 23; Psalm 79; Proverbs 25:21-23; Daniel 6; Luke 17; Acts 14
Ephesians 6:17 Lord, I take up the sword of the Spirit, which is your word. Help me to. Your word "is quick and powerful, and sharper than any two edged sword, piercing even to the dividing asunder of soul and spirit, and of the joints and marrow, and is a discerner of the thoughts and intents of the heart." (Hebrews 4:12). You've also said that your word will not return unto you "void, but it shall accomplish that which" you "please, and it shall prosper in the thing whereto" you "sent it." (Isaiah 55:11) May I use your word effectively, in a way that honors you, my Lord and my God.

October 19
II Kings 24-25; Psalm 80; Proverbs 25:24-25; Daniel 7; Luke 18; Acts 15
Ephesians 6:16 Lord, I take up the shield of faith, by which I may quench all the fiery darts of the wicked. Help me to. I know that "without faith it is impossible to please" you (Hebrews 11:6). Thank you for giving me faith in you. You are worthy of all faith. When the enemy of my soul tries to wound me, I turn to you in faith, knowing that you are God All Mighty, and he is not. You are in control. You have a plan. You will accomplish your plan. You are a good God. Your arm is not shortened. You will succeed in doing your will. The enemy of my soul will fail. I put my trust in You.

October 20
I Chronicles 1; Psalm 81; Proverbs 25:26-28; Daniel 8; Luke 19; Acts 16
Ephesians 6:17 Lord, I wear the helmet of salvation. Help me to. Thank you so very much for saving me, Lord. I get to spend eternity with you! What could possibly compare with that? Just as a physical helmet protects the head, I ask that your salvation protects my mind. You have "not given us the spirit of fear; but of power, and of love, and of a sound mind. (II Timothy 1:7) And as I "have the mind of Christ" (I Corinthians 2:16), help me to use it for your glory.

October 21
I Chronicles 2; Psalm 82; Proverbs 26:1-2; Daniel 9; Luke 20; Acts 17
Ephesians 6:18 Lord I pray in the spirit with all prayer and supplication. Help me to. Thank you so much for prayer. I get to talk with the king of Kings and lord of Lords! I get to talk with All Mighty God! And you delight to hear me. I am unworthy. Thank you for Jesus. Thank you that He made it possible for me to come to you in prayer. Teach me to pray, Lord.

October 22
I Chronicles 3; Psalm 83; Proverbs 26:3-5; Daniel 10; Luke 21; Acts 18
Ephesians 6:14 Lord, I put on the breastplate of righteousness. Help me to. No matter what anyone says, no matter how often I fail, I wear your righteousness, because Jesus' blood has washed me of all my sin. I stand before you completely righteous, because of Jesus.

October 23
I Chronicles 4; Psalm 84; Proverbs 26:6-7; Daniel 11; Luke 22; Acts 19
Ephesians 6:14 Lord I put on the belt of truth. Help me to. You call yourself the truth. You call the enemy of our souls the father of lies. I choose truth. I will walk in truth, because you are truth. The truth is: you are God, I am not. You sent your son to save the world—and that includes me—out of love. Jesus paid for my sins on the cross. The truth is: You love me. And you have provided salvation for me. You have plans for me—good plans—not evil plans. You always provide for me. And you have work for me to do, telling others about you, making disciples. The truth is, because Jesus has washed my sins away, I get to spend eternity in your wonderful presence. In the light of all that, no matter what happens, I will stand firm and not be defeated.

October 24
I Chronicles 5; Psalm 85; Proverbs 26:8-10; Daniel 12; Luke 23; Acts 20
Ephesians 6:15 Lord, I wear the preparation of the Gospel of Peace. Help me to. Help me to recognize the opportunities you set before me to spread your Gospel of Peace. Help me to take courage and do it. Please give me creative ways to do this. Help me to see these souls as you see them. May I be prepared to tell them of the hope that lies in me. Help me to "study to show myself approved unto God, a workman that needeth not to be ashamed, rightly dividing the word of truth." (II Timothy 2:15) May I do all in my power to be prepared. And may you do all that isn't in my power to make me prepared with the Gospel of Peace.

October 25
I Chronicles 6; Psalm 86; Proverbs 26:11-12; Hosea 1; Luke 24; Acts 21
Ephesians 6:17 Lord, I take up the sword of the Spirit, which is your word. Help me to. Your word "is quick and powerful, and sharper than any two edged sword, piercing even to the dividing asunder of soul and spirit, and of the joints and marrow, and is a discerner of the thoughts and intents of the heart." (Hebrews 4:12). You've also said that your word will not return unto you "void, but it shall accomplish that which" you "please, and it shall prosper in the thing whereto" you "sent it." (Isaiah 55:11) May I use your word effectively, in a way that honors you, my Lord and my God.

October 26
I Chronicles 7; Psalm 87; Proverbs 26:13-15; Hosea 2; Acts 22
Ephesians 6:16 Lord, I take up the shield of faith, by which I may quench all the fiery darts of the wicked. Help me to. I know that "without faith it is impossible to please" you (Hebrews 11:6). Thank you for giving me faith in you. You are worthy of all faith. When the enemy of my soul tries to wound me, I turn to you in faith, knowing that you are God All Mighty, and he is not. You are in control. You have a plan. You will accomplish your plan. You are a good God. Your arm is not shortened. You will succeed in doing your will. The enemy of my soul will fail. I put my trust in You.

October 27
I Chronicles 8; Psalm 88; Proverbs 26:16-17; Hosea 3; Acts 23
Ephesians 6:17 Lord, I wear the helmet of salvation. Help me to. Thank you so very much for saving me, Lord. I get to spend eternity with you! What could possibly

compare with that? Just as a physical helmet protects the head, I ask that your salvation protects my mind. You have "not given us the spirit of fear; but of power, and of love, and of a sound mind. (II Timothy 1:7) And as I "have the mind of Christ" (I Corinthians 2:16), help me to use it for your glory.

October 28
I Chronicles 9; Psalm 89; Proverbs 26:18-20; Hosea 4; Acts 24
Ephesians 6:18 Lord I pray in the spirit with all prayer and supplication. Help me to. Thank you so much for prayer. I get to talk with the king of Kings and lord of Lords! I get to talk with All Mighty God! And you delight to hear me. I am unworthy. Thank you for Jesus. Thank you that He made it possible for me to come to you in prayer. Teach me to pray, Lord.

October 29
I Chronicles 10-11; Psalm 90; Proverbs 26:21-23; Hosea 5; Acts 25
Ephesians 6:13-18 Lord, I put on the whole armor of God. Please help me to. I put on the breastplate of righteousness, and the belt of truth. On my feet I wear the preparation of the Gospel of Peace. I take up the sword of the Spirit, which is the word of God, and the shield of faith, by which I may quench all the fiery darts of the wicked. I wear the helmet of salvation. I pray in the Spirit with all prayer and supplication. And having done all, I will stand.

October 30
I Chronicles 12; Psalm 91; Proverbs 26:24-26; Hosea 6; Acts 26
"For the weapons of our warfare are not carnal, but mighty through God to the pulling down of strongholds; casting down imaginations, and every high thing that exalteth itself against the knowledge of God, and bringing into captivity every thought to the obedience o Christ." (I Corinthians 10:4-5)

October 31
I Chronicles 13-14; Psalm 92; Proverbs 26:27-28; Hosea 7; Acts 27
I "put on the armor of light" and "walk honestly, as in the day; not in rioting and drunkenness, not in chambering and wantonness, not in strife and envying." But I put "on the Lord Jesus Christ, and make not provision for the flesh, to fulfill the lusts thereof." (Romans 13:12-14)

November 1
I Chronicles 15; Psalm 93; Proverbs 27:1-3; Hosea 8; Acts 28
Prayer for me to be a good wife/husband/family member to my spouse/family member.

November 2
I Chronicles 16; Psalm 94; Proverbs 27:4-5; Hosea 9; Hebrews 1
Prayer for my spouse/family member to be a good wife/husband/family member to me. (Praying for, not against, my beloved one.)

November 3
I Chronicles 17-18; Psalm 95; Proverbs 27:6-9; Hosea 10; Hebrews 2
Ephesians 3:16-19 Lord, I pray that you grant my beloved, according to the riches of your glory, to be strengthened with might by your Spirit in my beloved's inner man; That Christ may dwell in my beloved's heart by faith; that he/she being rooted and grounded in love, may be able to comprehend with all saints what is the breadth and length, and depth, and height; And to know the love of Christ, which passeth knowledge, that he/she might be filled with all the fullness of God.

November 4
I Chronicles 19-20; Psalm 96; Proverbs 27:10-12; Hosea 11; Hebrews 3

Philippians 1:10-11 I pray that my beloved's love may abound in knowledge and all judgment—that he/she may test and assess all things according to excellence—that he/she may be sincere and not hypocritical and that he/she won't cause anyone to stumble—and that he/she will be filled with the fruits of righteousness.

November 5
I Chronicles 21-22; Psalm 97; Proverbs 27:13-14; Hosea 12; Hebrews 4
"I will praise thee, O Lord, with my whole heart; I will show forth all of thy marvelous works. I will be glad and rejoice in thee: I will sing praise to thy name, O thou most high." (Psalm 9:1&2)

November 6
I Chronicles 23-24; Psalm 98; Proverbs 27:15-17; Hosea 13; Hebrews 5
Hebrews 4:14-16 "Seeing then that we have a great high priest, that is passed into the Heavens, Jesus the Son of God, let us hold fast our profession. For we have not an high priest which cannot be touched with the feeling of our infirmities; but was in all points tempted like as we are, yet without sin. Let us therefore come boldly unto the throne of grace, that we may obtain mercy, and find grace to help in time of need."

November 7
I Chronicles 25; Psalm 99; Proverbs 27:18-20; Hosea 14; Hebrews 6
Isaiah 65:24 "And it shall come to pass, that before they call, I will answer; and while they are yet speaking I will hear."

November 8
I Chronicles 26; Psalm 100; Proverbs 27:21-22; Joel 1; Hebrews 7
Prayer for me to be a good wife/husband/family member to my spouse/family member.

November 9
I Chronicles 27; Psalm 101; Proverbs 27:23-25; Joel 2; Hebrews 8
Prayer for my spouse/family member to be a good wife/husband/family member to me. (Praying *for*, not *against*, my beloved one.)

November 10
I Chronicles 28; Psalm 102; Proverbs 27:26-27; Joel 3; Hebrews 9
Ephesians 3:16-19 Lord, I pray that you grant my beloved, according to the riches of your glory, to be strengthened with might by your Spirit in my beloved's inner man; That Christ may dwell in my beloved's heart by faith; that he/she being rooted and grounded in love, may be able to comprehend with all saints what is the breadth and length, and depth, and height; And to know the love of Christ, which passeth knowledge, that he/she might be filled with all the fullness of God.

November 11
I Chronicles 29; Psalm 103; Proverbs 28:1-3; Amos 1; Hebrews 10
Philippians 1:10-11 I pray that my beloved's love may abound in knowledge and all judgment—that he/she may test and assess all things according to excellence—that he/she may be sincere and not hypocritical and that he/she won't cause anyone to stumble—and that he/she will be filled with the fruits of righteousness.

November 12
II Chronicles 1-2; Psalm 104; Proverbs 28:4-5; Amos 2; Hebrews 11
"I will praise thee, O Lord, with my whole heart; I will show forth all of they marvelous works. I will be glad and rejoice in thee: most high." (Psalm 9:1&2)

November 13
II Chronicles 3-4; Psalm 105; Proverbs 28:6-7; Amos 3; Hebrews 12
Hebrews 4:14-16 "Seeing then that we have a great high priest, that is passed into the Heavens, Jesus the Son of God, let us hold fast our profession. For we have not an

high priest which cannot be touched with the feeling of our infirmities; but was in all points tempted like as we are, yet without sin. Let us therefore come boldly unto the throne of grace, that we may obtain mercy, and find grace to help in time of need."

November 14
II Chronicles 5; Psalm 106; Proverbs 28:8-10; Amos 4; Hebrews 13
Isaiah 65:24 "And it shall come to pass, that before they call, I will answer; and while they are yet speaking I will hear."

November 15
II Chronicles 6; Psalm 107; Proverbs 28:11; Amos 5; John 1
Prayer for me to be a good wife/husband/family member to my spouse/family member.

November 16
II Chronicles 7-8; Psalm 108; Proverbs 28:12; Amos 6; John 2
Prayer for my spouse/family member to be a good wife/husband/family member to me. (Praying *for*, not *against*, my beloved one.)

November 17
II Chronicles 9-10; Psalm 109; Proverbs 28:13; Amos 7; John 3
Ephesians 3:16-19 Lord, I pray that you grant my beloved, according to the riches of your glory, to be strengthened with might by your Spirit in my beloved's inner man; That Christ may dwell in my beloved's heart by faith; that he/she being rooted and grounded in love, may be able to comprehend with all saints what is the breadth and length, and depth, and height; And to know the love of Christ, which passeth knowledge, that he/she might be filled with all the fullness of God.

November 18
II Chronicles 11-12; Psalm 110; Proverbs 28:14; Amos 8; John 4
Philippians 1:10-11 I pray that my beloved's love may abound in knowledge and all judgment—that he/she may test and assess all things according to excellence—that he/she may be sincere and not hypocritical and that he/she won't cause anyone to stumble—and that he/she will be filled with the fruits of righteousness.

November 19
II Chronicles 13-14; Psalm 111; Proverbs 28:15; Amos 9; John 5; James 1
"I will praise thee, O Lord, with my whole heart; I will show forth all of thy marvelous works. I will be glad and rejoice in thee: I will sing praise to thy name, O thou most high." (Psalm 9:1&2)

November 20
II Chronicles 15-16; Psalm 112; Proverbs 28:16; Obadiah ; John 6; James 2
Hebrews 4:14-16 "Seeing then that we have a great high priest, that is passed into the Heavens, Jesus the Son of God, let us hold fast our profession. For we have not an high priest which cannot be touched with the feeling of our infirmities; but was in all points tempted like as we are, yet without sin. Let us therefore come boldly unto the throne of grace, that we may obtain mercy, and find grace to help in time of need."

November 21
II Chronicles 17-18; Psalm 113; Proverbs 28:17; Jonah 1; John 7; James 3
Isaiah 65:24 "And it shall come to pass, that before they call, I will answer; and while they are yet speaking I will hear."

November 22
II Chronicles 19-20; Psalm 114; Proverbs 28:18; Jonah 2; John 8; James 4
Prayer for me to be a good wife/husband/family member to my spouse/family member.

November 23
II Chronicles 21-22; Psalm 115; Proverbs 28:19; Jonah 3; John 9; James 5

Prayer for my spouse/family member to be a good wife/husband/family member to me. (Praying *for*, not *against*, my beloved one.)

November 24

II Chronicles 23-24; Psalm 116; Proverbs 28:20; Jonah 4; John 10; I Peter 1

Ephesians 3:16-19 Lord, I pray that you grant my beloved, according to the riches of your glory, to be strengthened with might by your Spirit in my beloved's inner man; That Christ may dwell in my beloved's heart by faith; that he/she being rooted and grounded in love, may be able to comprehend with all saints what is the breadth and length, and depth, and height; And to know the love of Christ, which passeth knowledge, that he/she might be filled with all the fullness of God.

November 25

II Chronicles 25-26; Psalm 117; Proverbs 28:21; Micah 1; John 11; I Peter 2

Philippians 1:10-11 I pray that my beloved's love may abound in knowledge and all judgment—that he/she may test and assess all things according to excellence—that he/she may be sincere and not hypocritical and that he/she won't cause anyone to stumble—and that he/she will be filled with the fruits of righteousness.

November 26

II Chronicles 27-28; Psalm 118; Proverbs 28:22; Micah 2; John 12; I Peter 3

"I will praise thee, O Lord, with my whole heart; I will show forth all of thy marvelous works. I will be glad and rejoice in thee: I will sing praise to thy name, O thou most high." (Psalm 9:1&2)

November 27

II Chronicles 29; Psalm 119:1-40; Proverbs 28:23-25; Micah 3; John 13; I Peter 4

Hebrews 4:14-16 "Seeing then that we have a great high priest, that is passed into the Heavens, Jesus the Son of God, let us hold fast our profession. For we have not an high priest which cannot be touched with the feeling of our infirmities; but was in all points tempted like as we are, yet without sin. Let us therefore come boldly unto the throne of grace, that we may obtain mercy, and find grace to help in time of need."

November 28

II Chronicles 30-31; Psalm 119:41-88; Proverbs 28:26-27; Micah 4; John 14; I Peter 5

Isaiah 65:24 "And it shall come to pass, that before they call, I will answer; and while they are yet speaking I will hear."

November 29

II Chronicles 32-33; Psalm 119:89-136; Proverbs 28:28; Micah 5; John 15; II Peter 1

Prayer for me to be a good wife/husband/family member to my spouse/family member.

November 30

II Chronicles 34-35; Psalm 119:137-176; Proverbs 29:1-5; Micah 6; John 16; II Peter 2

Prayer for my spouse/family member to be a good wife/husband/family member to me. (Praying *for*, not *against*, my beloved one.)

December 1

II Chronicles 36; Psalm 120; Proverbs 29:6-7; Micah 7; John 17; II Peter 3

(Proverbs 31:10-13) "Who can find a virtuous woman? for her price is far above rubies. The heart of her husband doth safely trust in her, so that he shall have no need of spoil. She will do him good and not evil all the days of her life. She seeketh wool, and flax, and worketh willingly with her hands." May I do my beloved good all my life and never evil. Help me to look for good things to do—servant things—and do them—willingly. Help me to know that if I am virtuous, I am worthy of being looked for, pursued by my beloved, and that I have value and am not a burden. Help me to be trustworthy—in reality and also in my beloved's mind.

December 2
Ezra 1:1-2:35; Psalm 121; Proverbs 29:8-10; Nahum 1 ; John 18; 1 John 1

(Proverbs 31:14) "She is like the merchants' ships; she bringeth her food from afar." Lord, help me to bear the qualities of a merchant ship, carrying things of value—not a garbage scow, which carried garbage. May all that I bring into conversation and all things in life be of value, and not detrimental. May I be personally involved and not expect another to do my part. May I not simply give orders, but bring in the things of value myself. May I be willing and able to bring these things of value from a distance if that's where they are.

December 3
Ezra 2:36-70; Psalm 122; Proverbs 29:11-12; Nahum 2; John 19; I John 2

Five things to pray for my beloved

December 4
Ezra 3-4; Psalm 123; Proverbs 29:13-15; Nahum 3; John 20; I John 3

Proverbs 31:15 "She riseth also while it is yet night, and giveth meat to her household, and a portion to her maidens." Lord, help me to be the kind of person who is willing to deprive myself in order that I may give. May I be willing to deny myself extra sleep when someone needs me to give to him/her. I understand that I must rest—but this proverbs 31 woman, after resting her body and mind and soul, got up at the point of having rested enough and denied herself the luxury of resting abundantly, because others had a need for her to get busy and give. May I be this way—resting according to wisdom, but not according to greed. And may I give this way too—according to wisdom and love, not according to greed and self-centeredness.

December 5
Ezra 5-6; Psalm 124; Proverbs 29:16-17; Habakkuk 1; John 21; I John 4

Proverbs 31:16 "She considereth a field, and buyeth it: with the fruit of her hands she planteth a vineyard." Help me Lord to give thought and consideration as to what you want me to do, and then put wings to my prayers and thoughts and consideration and do what is in my power to make it happen. And then when it happens, help me to be busy about the work. The proverbs 31 woman thought about it, then bought it, then began using it. It was aimed at fruit-bearing—in her case: grapes. May I aim for fruit-bearing. It may not be a physical piece of land and vineyard, but please open my eyes and means to considering and buying and planting whatever "piece of land" You desire for me to.

December 6
Ezra 7; Psalm 125; Proverbs 29:18-20; Habakkuk 2; I John 5

Five things to pray for my beloved

December 7
Ezra 8; Psalm 126; Proverbs 29:21-22; Habakkuk 3; II John

Proverbs 31:17 "She girdeth her loins with strength, and strengtheneth her arms." Help me Lord, to put on strength and so *be* strength. If I don't do what I can, which is to put strength on—to latch hold of it and make it part of me—how can I expect to be strong? Help me to cover myself with strength, especially those parts of me that no one else sees. If I strengthen those secret parts of me and my life, those parts of me and my life that others see will also be strengthened. Help me, Lord—make me to be strong, both in secret and in public.

December 8
Ezra 9; Psalm 127; Proverbs 29:23-25; Zephaniah 1; III John

Proverbs 31:18 "She perceiveth that her merchandise is good: her candle goeth not out by night." Lord, help me to perceive correctly and be perceived correctly. I need not worry that the truth shines forth when I have given my best—when I have labored as I should, not being lazy. Then I know that what I have to contribute is good, for I have done my best. So Lord, help me to labor for you, giving you my best—faithfully—even when it costs me.

December 9
Ezra 10; Psalm 128; Proverbs 29:26-27; Zephaniah 2; Jude
Five things to pray for my beloved

December 10
Nehemiah 1; Psalm 129; Proverbs 30:1-3; Zephaniah 3; Revelation 1
Proverbs 31:19 "She layeth her hands to the spindle, and her hands hold the distaff." Lord help me to begin and then to continue on in whatever you call me to do. May I be willing to get personally involved—laying my hands on this work—touching it myself—pressing into it in commitment as I hold it and so make it mine—my work for Your glory, which is really Yours entrusted to me. May I do what You set before me to do.

December 11
Nehemiah 2; Psalm 130; Proverbs 30:4-6; Haggai 1; Revelation 2
Proverbs 31:20 "She stretcheth out her hand to the poor; yea, she reacheth forth her hands to the needy." Help me Lord, to live a life that is purposely reaching out to those in need—personally reaching out—not *only* writing a check for those who reach out, but in addition to writing a check, to do this *myself* also. Help me to touch—that personal involvement—the poor and the needy. Help me to see who are poor and who are needy and not just assume that I know already. Some have needs that go beyond money. Some are poor even though they have thousands in the bank. Help me to reach out to them.

December 12
Nehemiah 3; Psalm 131 Proverbs 30:7-10; Haggai 2; Revelation 3
Five things to pray for my beloved

December 13
Nehemiah 4; Psalm 132; Proverbs 30:11-14; Zechariah 1; Revelation 4
Proverbs 31:21 "She is not afraid of the snow for her household: for all her household are clothed with scarlet." Lord, help me to live my life in such a way that I will have no reason to fear for my household, no matter what comes. As much as depends on me, may I be faithful to do it, and leave the rest in Your hands, that I be not afraid for my household, knowing that I have done my part, and that You will do Yours. Thank You Lord.

December 14
Nehemiah 5; Psalm 133; Proverbs 30:15-17; Zechariah 2; Revelation 5
Proverbs 31:22 "She maketh herself coverings of tapestry; her clothing is silk and purple." Help me, Lord, to make things with my own hands and give it my best. This proverbs 31 woman made clothing for herself and it was the best. It was silk and the sought-after, valuable "purple". Help me to remember that it's alright if I have something of value and that it's alright to spend time on making something for me. Help me not to confuse a servant's heart with thinking I'm of no value. You gave Your Son for me, showing me that You find me valuable. Thank You Lord.

December 15
Nehemiah 6; Psalm 134; Proverbs 30:18-20; Zechariah 3; Revelation 6
Five things to pray for my beloved

December 16
Nehemiah 7; Psalm 135; Proverbs 30:21-23; Zechariah 4; Revelation 7
Proverbs 31:23 "Her husband is known in the gates, when he sitteth among the elders of the land." Lord may my life be lived in such a way that I not only bring glory to You, but also to my beloved, especially when he/she is out and about in the public eye. May he/she be known in a good and positive way, among those who have wisdom and authority. And may I have a hand in this, doing all in my power to promote him/her—ultimately for Your honor and glory, but also for my beloved's.

December 17
Nehemiah 8; Psalm 136; Proverbs 30:24-28; Zechariah 5; Revelation 8
Proverbs 31:24 "She maketh fine linen, and selleth it; and delivereth girdles unto the merchant." Lord, help me to make whatever You've given me the talent and means of making. And may I do it for Your glory. But may I not stop there, but take it to the next step and sell it—whether literally or figuratively—receiving from the blessings You mean for me to have from it. And may I use these blessings the way You intend. And finally, help me to deliver to others whatever it is You've given me the ability to do and make, that the blessings will not stop, but will be passed along. Help me to give You my best.

December 18
Nehemiah 9; Psalm 137; Proverbs 30:29-31; Zechariah 6; Revelation 9
Five things to pray for my beloved

December 19
Nehemiah 10; Psalm 138; Proverbs 30:32-33; Zechariah 7; Revelation 10
Proverbs 31:25 "Strength and honor are her clothing; and she shall rejoice in time to come." Lord, help me to be the person You created me to be. May I be a person of strength and honor. May my strength and honor cover me like clothing covers my body—touching all of me—covering what is private, but not taking it away—enhancing what is public, giving it beauty and grace and an artistic look. May my strength and honor be in You. The joy of the Lord is my strength (Nehemiah 8:10). And being clothed in strength and honor, may I rejoice. Even if today is hard, help me to remember that I will rejoice in time to come—for "weeping may endure for a night, but joy cometh in the morning." (Psalm 30:5)

December 20
Nehemiah 11; Psalm 139; Proverbs 31:1-3; Zechariah 8; Revelation 11
Proverbs 31:26 "She openeth her mouth with wisdom; and in her tongue is the law of kindness." Lord, may I have a kind tongue and use it wisely. May I remember to use it and not stay silent all the time. But in using it, may I use wisdom and kindness—both of which know that there is a right timing and a right choice of words and tone of voice that when all combined together make for wise and kind speech. Help me so to speak.

December 21
Nehemiah 12; Psalm 140; Proverbs 31:4-9; Zechariah 9; Revelation 12
Five things to pray for my beloved

December 22
Nehemiah 13; Psalm 141; Proverbs 31:10-12; Zechariah 10; Revelation 13
Proverbs 31:27 "She looketh well to the ways of her household, and eateth not the bread of idleness." Lord, help me to be observant where my household is concerned. Help me to purposefully look and notice everything that concerns my household. And may I not stop with the looking and observing, but may I act upon what I observe and

not be idle. May I not allow things to slip by. But may I do what needs to be done, even when I don't feel like it for one reason or another. Help me not to cultivate idleness.

December 23

Esther 1; Psalm 142; Proverbs 31:13-15; Zechariah 11; Revelation 14

Proverbs 31:28 "Her children arise up, and call her blessed; her husband also, and he praiseth her." Whether children of my body or children of my ministry, or children of my heart, whether they are near or far, teach me how to pray in regard to them. Lord may I live every day in such a way as being deserving of having the children rise up and call me blessed.

December 24

Esther 2; Psalm 143; Proverbs 31:16-18; Zechariah 12; Revelation 15

Five things to pray for my beloved

December 25

Matthew 1:18-2:23; Luke 2:1-20

Proverbs 31:28 "Her children arise up, and call her blessed; her husband also, and he praiseth her." May I *be* all that I am supposed to be, so as to be deserving of my beloved's praise and the children's blessings—whether or not they give it to me. Please help me to live so closely to You that I will be deserving of their blessings and praises, but not worry about whether or not they give it to me. May I leave that to be between You and them. And may I be willing to give my beloved and my parents praise and blessings.

December 26

Esther 3; Psalm 144-145; Proverbs 31:19-21; Zechariah 13; Revelation 16

Proverbs 31:29 "Many daughters have done virtuously, but thou excellest them all." Lord, when all is said and done, all that is going to matter is You and how we lived virtuously. May I live my life virtuously for You. May I do such a good job at it, that when compared to others, I will excel them all—not so that I can be number one—but that my aim will be to be as virtuous as You created me to be—and that all of us will so strive. May I succeed, Lord. May I not see myself as a failure and as less, but as one who is virtuous—and this is the place of excelling them all: in virtue. May I never forget the value of virtue.

December 27

Esther 4; Psalm 146; Proverbs 31:22-23; Zechariah 14; Revelation 17

Five things to pray for my beloved

December 28

Esther 5; Psalm 147; Proverbs 31:24-25; Malachi 1; Revelation 18

Proverbs 31:30 "Favor is deceitful, and beauty is vain: but a woman that feareth the LORD, she shall be praised." Lord, help me to discern between what is real and what is empty. May I not concentrate on illusions like favor and beauty. At best, these are only momentary. But instead, may I spend my life and all that I am and have in fearing You—holding You in awesome esteem, for You are my God. And may I allow this very thing to be my praise.

December 29

Esther 6-7; Psalm 148; Proverbs 31:26-27; Malachi 2; Revelation 19

Proverbs 31:31 "Give her of the fruit of her hands; and let her own works praise her in the gates." Lord, please give me fruit. You've promised that the righteous will still bear fruit in old age (Psalm 92:14). This is my heart's desire—that I will never stop bearing fruit unto You until you call me home. May this fruit be my praise—not *me* but my *fruit*. May my fruit take me to the places of influence, wherever You would have me to go.

December 30
Esther 8; Psalm 149; Proverbs 31:28-29; Malachi 3; Revelation 20
Five things to pray for my beloved
December 31
Esther 9-10; Psalm 150; Proverbs 31:30-31; Malachi 4; Revelation 21-22
Five things to pray for my beloved

Verses to Memorize
The following are in the King James Version[ii]

Salvation Verses:
For God so loved the world, that he gave his only begotten Son, that whosoever believeth in him should not perish, but have everlasting life.
(John 3:16)
For all have sinned, and come short of the glory of God;
(Romans 3:23)
The wages of sin is death; but the gift of God is eternal life through Jesus Christ our Lord.
(Romans 6:23)
Believe on the Lord Jesus Christ and thou shalt be saved, and thy house
(Acts 16:31)

For by grace are ye saved through faith; and that not of yourselves: it is the gift of God: not of works, lest any man should boast.
(Ephesians 2:8-9)
As it is written, There is none righteous, no, not one.
(Romans 3:10)
If we confess our sins, he is faithful and just to forgive us our sins, and to cleanse us from all unrighteousness.
(I John 1:9)
Turn ye, turn ye from your evil ways; for why will ye die?
(Ezekiel 33:11)
Now is the accepted time; behold, now is the day of salvation.
(II Corinthians 6:2)
For God sent not his Son into the world to condemn the world; but that the world through him might be saved.
(John 3:17)
For with the heart man believeth unto righteousness, and with
For whosoever shall call upon the name of the Lord shall be saved.
(Romans 10:13)

Verses to Encourage Faith:
Hebrews 11:1-40; 12:1-2

[11:1] Now faith is the substance of things hoped for, the evidence of things not seen.

[2] For by it the elders obtained a good report.

[3] Through faith we understand that the worlds were framed by the word of God, so that things which are seen were not made of things which do appear.

[4] By faith Abel offered unto God a more excellent sacrifice than Cain, by which he obtained witness that he was righteous, God testifying of his gifts: and by it he being dead yet speaketh.

[5] By faith Enoch was translated that he should not see death; and was not found, because God had translated him: for before his translation he had this testimony, that he pleased God.

[6] But without faith it is impossible to please him: for he that cometh to God must believe that he is, and that he is a rewarder of them that diligently seek him.

[7] By faith Noah, being warned of God of things not seen as yet, moved with fear, prepared an ark to the saving of his house; by the which he condemned the world, and became heir of the righteousness which is by faith.

[8] By faith Abraham, when he was called to go out into a place which he should after receive for an inheritance, obeyed; and he went out, not knowing whither he went.

[9] By faith he sojourned in the land of promise, as in a strange country, dwelling in tabernacles with Isaac and Jacob, the heirs with him of the same promise:

[10] For he looked for a city which hath foundations, whose builder and maker is God.

[11] Through faith also Sara herself received strength to conceive seed, and was delivered of a child when she was past age, because she judged him faithful who had promised.

[12] Therefore sprang there even of one, and him as good as dead, so many as the stars of the sky in multitude, and as the sand which is by the sea shore innumerable.

[13] These all died in faith, not having received the promises, but having seen them afar off, and were persuaded of them, and embraced them, and confessed that they were strangers and pilgrims on the earth.

[14] For they that say such things declare plainly that they seek a country.

[15] And truly, if they had been mindful of that country from whence they came out, they might have had opportunity to have returned.

[16] But now they desire a better country, that is, an heavenly: wherefore God is not ashamed to be called their God: for he hath prepared for them a city.

[17] By faith Abraham, when he was tried, offered up Isaac: and he that had received the promises offered up his only begotten son,

[18] Of whom it was said, That in Isaac shall thy seed be called:

[19] Accounting that God was able to raise him up, even from the dead; from whence also he received him in a figure.

[20] By faith Isaac blessed Jacob and Esau concerning things to come.

[21] By faith Jacob, when he was a dying, blessed both the sons of Joseph; and worshipped, leaning upon the top of his staff.

[22] By faith Joseph, when he died, made mention of the departing of the children of Israel; and gave commandment concerning his bones.

[23] By faith Moses, when he was born, was hid three months of his parents, because they saw he was a proper child; and they were not afraid of the king's commandment.

[24] By faith Moses, when he was come to years, refused to be called the son of Pharaoh's daughter;

[25] Choosing rather to suffer affliction with the people of God, than to enjoy the pleasures of sin for a season;

[26] Esteeming the reproach of Christ greater riches than the treasures in Egypt: for he had respect unto the recompence of the reward.

[27] By faith he forsook Egypt, not fearing the wrath of the king: for he endured, as seeing him who is invisible.

[28] Through faith he kept the passover, and the sprinkling of blood, lest he that destroyed the firstborn should touch them.

[29] By faith they passed through the Red sea as by dry land: which the Egyptians assaying to do were drowned.

[30] By faith the walls of Jericho fell down, after they were compassed about seven days.

[31] By faith the harlot Rahab perished not with them that believed not, when she had received the spies with peace.

[32] And what shall I more say? for the time would fail me to tell of Gedeon, and of Barak, and of Samson, and of Jephthae; of David also, and Samuel, and of the prophets:

[33] Who through faith subdued kingdoms, wrought righteousness, obtained promises, stopped the mouths of lions,

[34] Quenched the violence of fire, escaped the edge of the sword, out of weakness were made strong, waxed valiant in fight, turned to flight the armies of the aliens.

[35] Women received their dead raised to life again: and others were tortured, not accepting deliverance; that they might obtain a better resurrection:

[36] And others had trial of cruel mockings and scourgings, yea, moreover of bonds and imprisonment:

[37] They were stoned, they were sawn asunder, were tempted, were slain with the sword: they wandered about in sheepskins and goatskins; being destitute, afflicted, tormented;

[38] (Of whom the world was not worthy:) they wandered in deserts, and in mountains, and in dens and caves of the earth.

[39] And these all, having obtained a good report through faith, received not the promise:

[40] God having provided some better thing for us, that they without us should not be made perfect.

[12:1] Wherefore seeing we also are compassed about with so great a cloud of witnesses, let us lay aside every weight, and the sin which doth so easily beset us, and let us run with patience the race that is set before us,

[2] Looking unto Jesus the author and finisher of our faith; who for the joy that was set before him endured the cross, despising the shame, and is set down at the right hand of the throne of God.

The Ten Commandments
Exodus 20:1-17

[20:1] And God spake all these words, saying

[2] I *am* the LORD thy God, which have brought thee out of the land of Egypt, out of the house of bondage.

[3] Thou shalt have no other gods before me.

[4] Thou shalt not make unto thee any graven image, or any likeness *of any thing* that *is* in heaven above, or that *is* in the earth beneath, or that *is* in the water under the earth:

[5] Thou shalt not bow down thyself to them, nor serve them: for I the LORD thy God *am* a jealous God, visiting the iniquity of the fathers upon the children unto the third and fourth *generation* of them that hate me;

[6] And shewing mercy unto thousands of them that love me, and keep my commandments.

[7] Thou shalt not take the name of the LORD thy God in vain; for the LORD will not hold him guiltless that taketh his name in vain.

[8] Remember the sabbath day, to keep it holy.

[9] Six days shalt thou labour, and do all thy work:

[10] But the seventh day *is* the sabbath of the LORD thy God: *in it* thou shalt not do any work, thou, nor thy son, nor thy daughter, thy manservant, nor thy maidservant, nor thy cattle, nor thy stranger that *is* within thy gates:

[11] For *in* six days the LORD made heaven and earth, the sea, and all that in them *is*, and rested the seventh day: wherefore the LORD blessed the sabbath day, and hallowed it.

[12] Honour thy father and thy mother: that thy days may be long upon the land which the LORD thy God giveth thee.

[13] Thou shalt not kill.

[14] Thou shalt not commit adultery.

[15] Thou shalt not steal.

[16] Thou shalt not bear false witness against thy neighbour.

[17] Thou shalt not covet thy neighbour's house, thou shalt not covet thy neighbour's wife, nor his manservant, nor his maidservant, nor his ox, nor his ass, nor any thing that *is* thy neighbour's.

Jesus' Sermon on the Mount Verses:
Matthew 5-7

[5:1] And seeing the multitudes, he went up into a mountain: and when he was set, his disciples came unto him: [2] And he opened his mouth, and taught them, saying,

[3] Blessed are the poor in spirit: for theirs is the kingdom of heaven. [4] Blessed are they that mourn: for they shall be comforted. [5] Blessed are the meek: for they shall inherit the earth. [6] Blessed are they which do hunger and thirst after righteousness: for they shall be filled. [7] Blessed are the merciful: for they shall obtain mercy. [8] Blessed are the pure in heart: for they shall see God. [9] Blessed are the peacemakers: for they shall be called the children of God. [10] Blessed are they which are persecuted for righteousness' sake: for theirs is the kingdom of heaven. [11] Blessed are ye, when men shall revile you, and persecute you, and shall say all manner of evil against you falsely, for my sake.

[12] Rejoice, and be exceeding glad: for great is your reward in heaven: for so persecuted they the prophets which were before you.

[13] Ye are the salt of the earth: but if the salt have lost his savour, wherewith shall it be salted? it is thenceforth good for nothing, but to be cast out, and to be trodden under foot of men. [14] Ye are the light of the world. A city that is set on an hill cannot be hid.

[15] Neither do men light a candle, and put it under a bushel, but on a candlestick; and it giveth light unto all that are in the house. [16] Let your light so shine before men, that they may see your good works, and glorify your Father which is in heaven.

[17] Think not that I am come to destroy the law, or the prophets: I am not come to destroy, but to fulfil. [18] For verily I say unto you, Till heaven and earth pass, one jot or one tittle shall in no wise pass from the law, till all be fulfilled. [19] Whosoever therefore

shall break one of these least commandments, and shall teach men so, he shall be called the least in the kingdom of heaven: but whosoever shall do and teach them, the same shall be called great in the kingdom of heaven. [20] For I say unto you, That except your righteousness shall exceed the righteousness of the scribes and Pharisees, ye shall in no case enter into the kingdom of heaven.

[21] Ye have heard that it was said by them of old time, Thou shalt not kill; and whosoever shall kill shall be in danger of the judgment: [22] But I say unto you, That whosoever is angry with his brother without a cause shall be in danger of the judgment: and whosoever shall say to his brother, Raca, shall be in danger of the council: but whosoever shall say, Thou fool, shall be in danger of hell fire. [23] Therefore if thou bring thy gift to the altar, and there rememberest that thy brother hath ought against thee; [24] Leave there thy gift before the altar, and go thy way; first be reconciled to thy brother, and then come and offer thy gift. [25] Agree with thine adversary quickly, whiles thou art in the way with him; lest at any time the adversary deliver thee to the judge, and the judge deliver thee to the officer, and thou be cast into prison. [26] Verily I say unto thee, Thou shalt by no means come out thence, till thou hast paid the uttermost farthing.

[27] Ye have heard that it was said by them of old time, Thou shalt not commit adultery: [28] But I say unto you, That whosoever looketh on a woman to lust after her hath committed adultery with her already in his heart. [29] And if thy right eye offend thee, pluck it out, and cast it from thee: for it is profitable for thee that one of thy members should perish, and not that thy whole body should be cast into hell. [30] And if thy right hand offend thee, cut it off, and cast it from thee: for it is profitable for thee that one of thy members should perish, and not that thy whole body should be cast into hell. [31] It hath been said, Whosoever shall put away his wife, let him give her a writing of divorcement: [32] But I say unto you, That whosoever shall put away his wife, saving for the cause of fornication, causeth her to commit adultery: and whosoever shall marry her that is divorced committeth adultery.

[33] Again, ye have heard that it hath been said by them of old time, Thou shalt not forswear thyself, but shalt perform unto the Lord thine oaths: [34] But I say unto you, Swear not at all; neither by heaven; for it is God's throne: [35] Nor by the earth; for it is his footstool: neither by Jerusalem; for it is the city of the great King. [36] Neither shalt thou swear by thy head, because thou canst not make one hair white or black. [37] But let your communication be, Yea, yea; Nay, nay: for whatsoever is more than these cometh of evil.

[38] Ye have heard that it hath been said, An eye for an eye, and a tooth for a tooth: [39] But I say unto you, That ye resist not evil: but whosoever shall smite thee on thy right cheek, turn to him the other also. [40] And if any man will sue thee at the law, and take away thy coat, let him have thy cloke also. [41] And whosoever shall compel thee to go a mile, go with him twain. [42] Give to him that asketh thee, and from him that would borrow of thee turn not thou away.

[43] Ye have heard that it hath been said, Thou shalt love thy neighbour, and hate thine enemy. [44] But I say unto you, Love your enemies, bless them that curse you, do good

to them that hate you, and pray for them which despitefully use you, and persecute you; [45] That ye may be the children of your Father which is in heaven: for he maketh his sun to rise on the evil and on the good, and sendeth rain on the just and on the unjust. [46] For if ye love them which love you, what reward have ye? do not even the publicans the same? [47] And if ye salute your brethren only, what do ye more than others? do not even the publicans so? [48] Be ye therefore perfect, even as your Father which is in heaven is perfect.

[6:1] Take heed that ye do not your alms before men, to be seen of them: otherwise ye have no reward of your Father which is in heaven. [2] Therefore when thou doest thine alms, do not sound a trumpet before thee, as the hypocrites do in the synagogues and in the streets, that they may have glory of men. Verily I say unto you, They have their reward. [3] But when thou doest alms, let not thy left hand know what thy right hand doeth: [4] That thine alms may be in secret: and thy Father which seeth in secret himself shall reward thee openly.

[5] And when thou prayest, thou shalt not be as the hypocrites are: for they love to pray standing in the synagogues and in the corners of the streets, that they may be seen of men. Verily I say unto you, They have their reward. [6] But thou, when thou prayest, enter into thy closet, and when thou hast shut thy door, pray to thy Father which is in secret; and thy Father which seeth in secret shall reward thee openly. [7] But when ye pray, use not vain repetitions, as the heathen do: for they think that they shall be heard for their much speaking. [8] Be not ye therefore like unto them: for your Father knoweth what things ye have need of, before ye ask him.

[9] After this manner therefore pray ye: Our Father which art in heaven, Hallowed be thy name. [10] Thy kingdom come. Thy will be done in earth, as it is in heaven. [11] Give us this day our daily bread. [12] And forgive us our debts, as we forgive our debtors. [13] And lead us not into temptation, but deliver us from evil: For thine is the kingdom, and the power, and the glory, for ever. Amen. [14] For if ye forgive men their trespasses, your heavenly Father will also forgive you: [15] But if ye forgive not men their trespasses, neither will your Father forgive your trespasses.

[16] Moreover when ye fast, be not, as the hypocrites, of a sad countenance: for they disfigure their faces, that they may appear unto men to fast. Verily I say unto you, They have their reward. [17] But thou, when thou fastest, anoint thine head, and wash thy face; [18] That thou appear not unto men to fast, but unto thy Father which is in secret: and thy Father, which seeth in secret, shall reward thee openly.

[19] Lay not up for yourselves treasures upon earth, where moth and rust doth corrupt, and where thieves break through and steal: [20] But lay up for yourselves treasures in heaven, where neither moth nor rust doth corrupt, and where thieves do not break through nor steal: [21] For where your treasure is, there will your heart be also. [22] The light of the body is the eye: if therefore thine eye be single, thy whole body shall be full of light. [23] But if thine eye be evil, thy whole body shall be full of darkness. If therefore the light that is in thee be darkness, how great is that darkness! [24] No man can serve

two masters: for either he will hate the one, and love the other; or else he will hold to the one, and despise the other. Ye cannot serve God and mammon.

[25] Therefore I say unto you, Take no thought for your life, what ye shall eat, or what ye shall drink; nor yet for your body, what ye shall put on. Is not the life more than meat, and the body than raiment? [26] Behold the fowls of the air: for they sow not, neither do they reap, nor gather into barns; yet your heavenly Father feedeth them. Are ye not much better than they? [27] Which of you by taking thought can add one cubit unto his stature? [28] And why take ye thought for raiment? Consider the lilies of the field, how they grow; they toil not, neither do they spin: [29] And yet I say unto you, That even Solomon in all his glory was not arrayed like one of these. [30] Wherefore, if God so clothe the grass of the field, which to day is, and to morrow is cast into the oven, shall he not much more clothe you, O ye of little faith? [31] Therefore take no thought, saying, What shall we eat? or, What shall we drink? or, Wherewithal shall we be clothed? [32] (For after all these things do the Gentiles seek:) for your heavenly Father knoweth that ye have need of all these things. [33] But seek ye first the kingdom of God, and his righteousness; and all these things shall be added unto you. [34] Take therefore no thought for the morrow: for the morrow shall take thought for the things of itself. Sufficient unto the day is the evil thereof.

[7:1] Judge not, that ye be not judged. [2] For with what judgment ye judge, ye shall be judged: and with what measure ye mete, it shall be measured to you again. [3] And why beholdest thou the mote that is in thy brother's eye, but considerest not the beam that is in thine own eye? [4] Or how wilt thou say to thy brother, Let me pull out the mote out of thine eye; and, behold, a beam is in thine own eye? [5] Thou hypocrite, first cast out the beam out of thine own eye; and then shalt thou see clearly to cast out the mote out of thy brother's eye. [6] Give not that which is holy unto the dogs, neither cast ye your pearls before swine, lest they trample them under their feet, and turn again and rend you.

[7] Ask, and it shall be given you; seek, and ye shall find; knock, and it shall be opened unto you: [8] For every one that asketh receiveth; and he that seeketh findeth; and to him that knocketh it shall be opened. [9] Or what man is there of you, whom if his son ask bread, will he give him a stone? [10] Or if he ask a fish, will he give him a serpent? [11] If ye then, being evil, know how to give good gifts unto your children, how much more shall your Father which is in heaven give good things to them that ask him?

[12] Therefore all things whatsoever ye would that men should do to you, do ye even so to them: for this is the law and the prophets. [13] Enter ye in at the strait gate: for wide is the gate, and broad is the way, that leadeth to destruction, and many there be which go in thereat: [14] Because strait is the gate, and narrow is the way, which leadeth unto life, and few there be that find it.

[15] Beware of false prophets, which come to you in sheep's clothing, but inwardly they are ravening wolves. [16] Ye shall know them by their fruits. Do men gather grapes of thorns, or figs of thistles? [17] Even so every good tree bringeth forth good fruit; but a corrupt tree bringeth forth evil fruit. [18] A good tree cannot bring forth evil fruit, neither

can a corrupt tree bring forth good fruit. [19] Every tree that bringeth not forth good fruit is hewn down, and cast into the fire. [20] Wherefore by their fruits ye shall know them.

[21] Not every one that saith unto me, Lord, Lord, shall enter into the kingdom of heaven; but he that doeth the will of my Father which is in heaven. [22] Many will say to me in that day, Lord, Lord, have we not prophesied in thy name? and in thy name have cast out devils? and in thy name done many wonderful works? [23] And then will I profess unto them, I never knew you: depart from me, ye that work iniquity. [24] Therefore whosoever heareth these sayings of mine, and doeth them, I will liken him unto a wise man, which built his house upon a rock: [25] And the rain descended, and the floods came, and the winds blew, and beat upon that house; and it fell not: for it was founded upon a rock. [26] And every one that heareth these sayings of mine, and doeth them not, shall be likened unto a foolish man, which built his house upon the sand: [27] And the rain descended, and the floods came, and the winds blew, and beat upon that house; and it fell: and great was the fall of it. [28] And it came to pass, when Jesus had ended these sayings, the people were astonished at his doctrine: [29] For he taught them as one having authority, and not as the scribes.

Verses for Worshipping God
Psalm 136:1-26

[136:1] O give thanks unto the LORD; for he is good: for his mercy endureth for ever.
[2] O give thanks unto the God of gods: for his mercy endureth for ever.
[3] O give thanks to the Lord of lords: for his mercy endureth for ever.
[4] To him who alone doeth great wonders: for his mercy endureth for ever.
[5] To him that by wisdom made the heavens: for his mercy endureth for ever.
[6] To him that stretched out the earth above the waters: for his mercy endureth for ever.
[7] To him that made great lights: for his mercy endureth for ever:
[8] The sun to rule by day: for his mercy endureth for ever:
[9] The moon and stars to rule by night: for his mercy endureth for ever.
[10] To him that smote Egypt in their firstborn: for his mercy endureth for ever:
[11] And brought out Israel from among them: for his mercy endureth for ever:
[12] With a strong hand, and with a stretched out arm: for his mercy endureth for ever.
[13] To him which divided the Red sea into parts: for his mercy endureth for ever:
[14] And made Israel to pass through the midst of it: for his mercy endureth for ever:
[15] But overthrew Pharaoh and his host in the Red sea: for his mercy endureth for ever.
[16] To him which led his people through the wilderness: for his mercy endureth for ever.
[17] To him which smote great kings: for his mercy endureth for ever:
[18] And slew famous kings: for his mercy endureth for ever:
[19] Sihon king of the Amorites: for his mercy endureth for ever:
[20] And Og the king of Bashan: for his mercy endureth for ever:
[21] And gave their land for an heritage: for his mercy endureth for ever:
[22] Even an heritage unto Israel his servant: for his mercy endureth for ever.

[23] Who remembered us in our low estate: for his mercy endureth for ever:

[24] And hath redeemed us from our enemies: for his mercy endureth for ever.

[25] Who giveth food to all flesh: for his mercy endureth for ever.

[26] O give thanks unto the God of heaven: for his mercy endureth for ever.

Verses on Love
I Corinthians 13:1-13

[13:1] Though I speak with the tongues of men and of angels, and have not charity[iii], I am become as sounding brass, or a tinkling cymbal.

[2] And though I have the gift of prophecy, and understand all mysteries, and all knowledge; and though I have all faith, so that I could remove mountains, and have not charity, I am nothing.

[3] And though I bestow all my goods to feed the poor, and though I give my body to be burned, and have not charity, it profiteth me nothing.

[4] Charity suffereth long, and is kind; charity envieth not;
charity vaunteth not itself, is not puffed up,

[5] Doth not behave itself unseemly, seeketh not her own, is not easily provoked, thinketh no evil;

[6] Rejoiceth not in iniquity, but rejoiceth in the truth;

[7] Beareth all things, believeth all things, hopeth all things, endureth all things.

[8] Charity never faileth: but whether there be prophecies, they shall fail; whether there be tongues, they shall cease; whether there be knowledge, it shall vanish away.

[9] For we know in part, and we prophesy in part.

[10] But when that which is perfect is come, then that which is in part shall be done away.

[11] When I was a child, I spake as a child, I understood as a child, I thought as a child: but when I became a man, I put away childish things.

[12] For now we see through a glass, darkly; but then face to face: now I know in part; but then shall I know even as also I am known.

[13] And now abideth faith, hope, charity, these three; but the greatest of these is charity.

Verses of Hope
John 14:1-3

[14:1] Let not your heart be troubled: ye believe in God, believe also in me.

[2] In my Father's house are many mansions: if it were not so, I would have told you. I go to prepare a place for you.

[3] And if I go and prepare a place for you, I will come again, and receive you unto myself; that where I am, there ye may be also.

"But these are written, that ye might believe that Jesus is the Christ, the Son of God; and that believing ye might have life through his name." John 20:31 (KJV)

"If we walk in the light, as he is in the light, we have fellowship one with another, and the blood of Jesus Christ his Son cleanseth us from all sin. If we say that we have no sin, we deceive ourselves, and the truth is not in us. If we confess our sins, he is faithful and just to forgive us our sins, and to cleanse us from all unrighteousness." I John 1:7-9 (KJV)

Books by Sally Demaray Hull
The Settlement-Book #1 of the series: The Documentary
New Settlers-Book #2 of the series: The Documentary
I Can't Remember My Past-Book #1 of the series: Amnesia Husband
I Can't Remember Your Name-Book #2 of the series: Amnesia Husband
I Can't Remember My Name-Book #3 of the series: Amnesia Husband
Shadow World-Book #1 of the series: Shadow World Quest-Seekers
The Quest-Book #2 of the series: Shadow World Quest Seekers
Shadow World Quest-Seekers Books 1 & 2-volumes 1 & 2 of series:
    Shadow World Quest-Seekers
Island Home
The Misfits of Callahan County-Book #1 of series: Misfits
Nobody Survived the Wilderness
Arena-Book #1 of the trilogy: The Nimbus Chronicles
Time Doors-Book #2 of the trilogy: The Nimbus Chronicles
Mulckite Peace Prince-Book #3 of the trilogy: The Nimbus Chronicles
The Trail Beyond-Book #1 of the series: Trails
Beyond the Trail-Book #2 of the series: Trails
The Timberton Trail-Book #3 of the series: Trails
War Trails-Book #4 of the series: Trails
The Shepherd's Trail-companion book of the series: Trails
Carolynn's Story-companion book of the series: Trails
Revenge at Two Feathers Mine-Book #1 of the trilogy: Schoolmarm
    Sheriff
My Husband's Dead Wife Lives-Book #2 of the trilogy: Schoolmarm
    Sheriff
Sheriff Husband and Deputy Wife-Book #3 of the trilogy: Schoolmarm
    Sheriff
Miss Brandt's Story-Companion book to the trilogy: Schoolmarm Sheriff
Fairy Tales and Shorts for Grownups Vol 1
Fairy Tales and Shorts for Grownups Vol 2
Two-D World
Mei Li of China Vol 1-Book #1 of the series: Y.O.U.T.H. A.T.M.
Mei Li of China Vol 2-Book #2 of the series: Y.O.U.T.H. A.T.M
Mei Li of China Vols 1 & 2-Books 1 & 2 of the series: Y.O.U.T.H. A.T.M.
That Truck Driver is My Dad-Book #3 of the series: Y.O.U.T.H. A.T.M.
Jayde
The Frog-Prince & I
Officer Material Vol 1-Book #1 of the series: Men of the Octofoil
Officer Material Vol 2-Book #2 of the series: Men of the Octofoil
Honor and Duty-Book #3 of the series: Men of the Octofoil
Upon Every Remembrance-Book #4 of the series: Men of the Octofoil
Eric's Dream-Book #5 of the series: Men of the Octofoil
The Wind and Waves-companion book of the series: Men of the
    Octofoil
Sensei—Teacher-companion book of the series: Men of the Octofoil

Ellen's Tears
Ellen's Journal – Chronological Edition
Ellen's Journal – Topical Edition
Ellen's China Vol 1
Ellen's China Vol 2
Did You To Go On The Same Trip: Australia by Charlie P. Hull Jr. and
    Sally Demaray Hull
Sally's Australian Journal 2009
Sally's Christmas Skits Vol 1
My Own Novel Blank Book 1
My Own Novel Blank Book With Lines 1
My Prayers Blank Book With Lines 1
My Conference Notes Blank Book With Lines 1
Tea With Jesus – Daily Bible Readings and Prayers
Tea With Jesus – Compact Edition of Daily Bible Readings and Prayers

By Charlie P. Hull Jr.
Over the Next Hill
Steps in the Dark of Light
Shade Tree 35
Memories of Dreams
Did You To Go On The Same Trip: Australia by Charlie P. Hull Jr. and
    Sally Demaray Hull

---

[i] All Scripture is quoted from the King James Version of the Bible.
Various word studies in this volume came from the efforts of Pastor Rick Johnson, using the following reference books: Strong's Concordance, Bauer/Arndt/Gingrich Word Studies, and Thayer's Word Studies.

[ii] All Scripture is quoted from the King James Version of the Bible.
Various word studies in this volume came from the efforts of Pastor Rick Johnson, using the following reference books: Strong's Concordance, Bauer/Arndt/Gingrich Word Studies, and Thayer's Word Studies.

[iii] The Greek word for charity means love

Made in the USA
Las Vegas, NV
15 December 2023

82901942R00039